7.60

Essay Index

DATE DUE

DEMCO, INC. 38-2931

SOME CONTEMPORARY NOVELISTS
(WOMEN)

SOME CONTEMPORARY NOVELISTS

(WOMEN)

BY

R. BRIMLEY JOHNSON

" Think of the real things, the deep things, the lonely frightened things in our souls."

Essay Index Reprint Series

Essay Index

BOOKS FOR LIBRARIES PRESS
FREEPORT, NEW YORK

First Published 1920
Reprinted 1967

INTERNATIONAL STANDARD BOOK NUMBER:
0-8369-0575-X

LIBRARY OF CONGRESS CATALOG CARD NUMBER:
67-26751

PRINTED IN THE UNITED STATES OF AMERICA

INTRODUCTION

INTRODUCTION

THIS volume is neither a judgment, a comparison, nor a prophecy. I do not affirm that the writers treated represent completely the work of women in fiction to-day; I would not assert, dogmatically, that theirs is even the *best* contemporary work : I have no desire to anticipate the judgment of posterity.

But just now they all count. They are conspicuously of the moment: keen to seize, and eager to present, the manifold currents of thought, experience, and philosophy, that make up the big wave of mental activity through which we have been hurried by war and its consequences. Inheriting those now far-off pre-war emotions and ideals amidst which we were all living (in normal sequence from Victorian placidity) ; they have "found themselves" during the upheaval, and they offer us their interpretations of new Truth.

Free and vital, curious and analytic, these women have read the "writing on the wall."

It would be extraordinarily difficult to deduce from these authors how far the war has influenced the art of fiction: but there is no doubt some analogy between their work and certain facts which have been maintained, with varying confidence at different times, by partial, or impartial, observers.

However temporary or limited its extent, either in the army itself or at home, there is too much evidence to altogether neglect or deny, that wave of religious revival or awakening to faith which did pass over mankind. Emphatically not for all men or at all times, but no less certainly in most unexpected quarters, a new spirituality arose among us to influence thought and emotion.

This movement was no doubt reflected in that hostility towards materialism which is obvious in much current fiction, that passionate search for Truth and Reality which characterises our most definitely advanced novelists.

The sudden, and startling, advance in the position of women was, naturally, not so new to women writers as to men: because it was, after all, merely the speeding of what their minds had been concentrated upon in the immediate pre-war days. The more thought-

ful, at least, were not unprepared, because
they had already given themselves to secure
it; and that restless hysteria (of which superficial observers made so much) was only
exhibited by those who before had been careless, indifferent, or prejudiced.

Women, of course, are no less than men,
alive to the dangers of forced progress. They
see that emancipation, suddenly acquired without effort, has produced in many a lack of heart
and conscience, which makes youth hard, and
is hurtful to middle-age. The new novelists,
on the whole, show themselves rather surpris-
ingly sympathetic to the parent, though only
Miss Fulton (and once Mrs. Mordaunt) have
used the particular problem as an occasion
for generalisation.

Social changes, again, are rather assumed
than dwelt upon, or made the subject of discussion; save that Miss Fulton, again, de-
claims, rather savagely, against the modern
lack of morality. The indifference to class
distinctions, and the decline of exclusiveness,
so apparent to-day, is simply taken for granted;
while our novelists are evidently quite aware
that even now all differences (which may, or
may not, mean superiority) are not wiped out
by material readjustment, or the extension of
opportunity. Such changes are not, moreover,

directly the outcome of war, which only pre-
cipitated what a spirit of liberalism and com-
monsense had been directed more gradually to
bring about.

As for what might, perhaps, be called local
colour, one is surprised, though perhaps without reason, to find the war so seldom apparent.
In many of these novels it is not mentioned,
or even in any way suggested. Yet the omission, perhaps, reveals true art; since, at least
to the new realist, the truth about human
nature is to be found in individual experience,
which depends upon our private relations to
each other, our loves, our hopes, our deaths,
and our despairs.

Miss Sinclair has, I think, met the apparent
omission most successfully in " The Tree of
Heaven," where she uses the war in every
chapter, and *yet* leaves us thinking and feeling
—*not* about the war (superficially and as a
problem in the world's history)—but about a
new group of intimate friends we are delighted
to know and proud to love: the more gratefully
because, despite the tragedy of their actual
experience, we find ourselves rather buoyed
up than depressed by the possibilities of hope
and happiness in human nature which they
reveal.

Miss Delafield's " War Workers " ; " Non-

Combatants," and "What Not," by Miss
Macaulay, and Miss Kaye-Smith's "Little
England," are all directly and exclusively
concerned with the actual social conditions of
these at home who "did their bit." Even
Miss Meynell makes one of her heroines take
up munitions, and in "Potterism" Miss
Macaulay completes her record by a post-
armistice picture of England.

But none of these seriously attack the complexities, social, national, and international;
save incidentally and as it were to illustrate
life on the surface and character as moulded
by special experience. They are of great value
historically, clever and sympathetic studies of
a unique era in the march of civilisation ; but
like all art most true in detail to its period they
lack permanence and universality. In a few
years they will seem more out of date than
other work by the same authors ; just as to-day
Dickens is more old-fashioned than Jane Austen, and Sheridan further away from us than
Shakespeare.

It is true that Miss Fulton attempts a far
more philosophical outlook, and discusses
many of the social and political questions involved: such as race differences, imperialism,
the new rich, and the psychology of war. But
I am disposed to regard her, at least in this

matter, as more than anything else an adept at catching the echoes of the moment: reproducing, with great skill and dramatic effect, what we all said and thought in the hurry of the moment, giving the absolutely contemporary view. This, again, has its historical value ; but it can scarcely be regarded as independent evidence towards any final conclusion.

Probably we should not expect, what certainly these women have not given us, any ordered philosophy or any final permanent revelation of the war-world as it was, or the new world as it may be. Some, indeed, claim to have learnt the truth from H. G. Wells, but I doubt if he has really disclosed it for more than quite a small section of humanity.

Each indeed follows her own line of thought, deduces her own philosophy. But it is possible to find similarities, and to establish comparisons, which lend at least some appearance of comprehensive unity within their reflections of Life and Man.

To begin with, (like the pioneers) women —however imaginative—have proved themselves to be essentially realistic. With one exception, they have also retained that most wise decision of Jane Austen and her early successors, to avow their sex always: writing

and reasoning, as women, without any attempt
to ape the male.

Though the suffrage (and all it implied) is
to them little more than a memory, they are
still at war with man—in so far as he clings
to the hearth-rug attitude of superiority.   Perhaps Miss Richardson, in her somewhat
spasmodic manner, brings this out most clearly.
She finds Man always a *poseur*, playing the
part expected of him, ruled by standards
largely inherited, seldom—if ever—facing the
Truth.   He has settled—once for all, it would
seem—what should, or should not, be done ;
even what should be thought about everything.
He will accept, indeed, new ideas.   His intellect is alert and receptive, broad-minded,
tolerant, even enterprising and adventurous.
He takes delight in all clever talk.   But the
soul of him stands still where it has always
stood :

"The knowledge of women is larger, bigger, deeper, less wordy and clever than
that of men.   .   .   .   Men have no real
knowledge   .   .   .   they do not understand
people."

"He could not be really happy with a
women unless he could also despise her
.   .   .   all men were like that in some way.
If a woman opposed them they went mad."

And again : " How utterly detestable mannish-
ness is ; so mighty and strong and comforting
when you have been mewed up with women
all your life, and then suddenly, in a second,
far away, utterly imbecile and aggravating with
a superior, self-satisfied smile because a woman
says one thing one minute and another the
next. Men ought to be horse-whipped, all
the grown men, all who have ever had that
self-satisfied smile, all, all, horsewhipped until
they apologise on their knees."

Even the commonplace Mrs. Lloyd-Evans
(in Miss Delafield's " Zella Sees Herself ")
is always declaring that " gentlemen do not
quite understand " : and Miss Amber Reeves
finds that it is by " their tiresome restlessness,
their curiosity, their disregard for security, for
seemliness, even for life itself, that men have
mastered the world and filled it with the wealth
of civilisation . . . that they have armed
the race with science, dignified it with art."

Whence the type—" Man with whose experiences women are trained to sympathise,
while he is not trained to sympathize with
theirs."

But the new woman, the feminine novelist
of the twentieth century, has abandoned the
old realism. She does not accept *observed*
revelation. She is seeking, with passionate

determination, for that Reality which is behind
the material, the things that matter, spiritual
things, ultimate Truth. And here she finds
man an outsider, wilfully blind, purposely indifferent. Not that her own conceptions, or
definitions, are yet by any means definite or
clearly formulated. Speaking generally, I
think one may say that she is striving to see
and express, all that part of life and humanity
which formal Religion once claimed to interpret : whether or no she elects to be called
religious, whether or no she seeks, or claims,
faith. This a new realism which, sternly rejecting the realist, looks through him to the
Real. For most of us, clearly, the influences
have been,—in the main,—unrecognised and
subconscious. The novelist is now concerned,
by presenting and analyzing them, to make us
realise their supreme importance. She will
unveil the mystery, bid us mark and learn.
To Miss Delafield's Zella it is Truth, to Miss
Richardson's Miriam it is Reality, Miss Stella
Benson finds it in fairyland. But, if their
nomenclature is individual, they all mean the
same thing.

In whatever directions the art of fiction may
ultimately develop, however new writers may
neglect tradition, there will remain a distinction, which is fundamental, between realism

and romance. In England, at any rate, the
realist arose with Richardson, following Defoe;
and his method (whether or not it were deliberately involved) was directed by observation, as the romantist had worked from an
ideal. He sought to copy, and reflect, real
life ; to draw men and women as they were ;
to re-create life and humanity. Success was
measured by the truth of his picture. This
was, in its origin, a healthy change, an advance
towards sanity and balance, because the ro-
mancers had wandered away from the legitimate exercise of their imagination, whereby
we reveal the beauty of an idealism which is
possible and true to nature. Seeking variety
from the more simple types of perfection, they
had invented a sort of morbid emotionalism,
wherein the over-refined, super-spiritual hero
and heroine struggled with utterly depraved
creatures—hating virtue, themselves impos-
sibly wicked. These guileless and beautiful
young darlings were fed on an emotional diet,
of which the ingredients had gradually become
more and more artificial ; they were false to
all practical morality, and in no way tended
to edification. The romance, in fact, had
become divorced from real life and human
nature. It was hopelessly morbid and pro-
foundly dull.

Richardson worked, carefully and conscientiously, on the opposite plan. He did not, indeed, escape propaganda or ignore virtue. He held up a mirror to the ideal. But it *was* a mirror, not a mere fancy-picture. Characters and plot alike were founded on fact, drawn from life, composed by observation. And this central conception of the realist—testing success in fiction by a comparison with reality—remained dominant in literature, despite the glorious romanticism of Scott and R. L. Stevenson's eloquent protests. Not that romance died. The opposition of ideas, indeed, took on a new form, so that, while writers of imagination were always colouring their pictures of life with ideals, always striving to show how much better and happier men might be than they actually were, the more literal and more determined realists came to exaggerate and pervert the truth, striving to shut out imagination.

Thus, in its turn, realism became false and artificial. Yielding to the tyranny of the materialist, novelists would now admit no truth outside appearances, what they could see and touch. They denied vision, till in the end they fell before that strange delusion of a decadent modernity : that all hope is blind, all beauty a veneer, all distinction between right and

2

wrong only cant. Truth, honest truth, must be ugly and can only breed despair. Whence, because convention (in real life) had wilfully hidden away certain social questions, the realist proclaimed the "problem," and there arose that intimate blending (which lapsed into identification) between realism and the sex, which (for a time) murdered art.

But to-day we are no longer materialistic. The limitations of science are freely admitted. The vision has returned. The younger women novelists of these latter days, no less free and truthful than their immediate predecessors, have discarded the dust and ashes. They are no longer content with what "just happens," or just how men look. They will not interpret old age by counting its wrinkles, or home-life by fly-stains on the wallpaper. They do not find all London at a night-club, or in the seats on the Embankment; all country-folk in the muck-heap. Their emotions are not all stirred by drugs and drabs. Yet they, too, are seeking for truth: and their courage is unflinching. Many, perhaps, are prepared to admit that they have not yet found her, only they know where to look. Beneath the surface, behind the veil, within the soul; there is a meaning. So far we accept romance: but we must take out, not put in; observe, not imagine; reveal, not

create.   This is the real realism ; to reflect
reality : the spiritual truth of things which is
life and character.   The new seekers are not
more afraid of pain and ugliness than the
problem-weavers ; they are no less resolute to
expose : but they also respect beauty and goodness, they know that it is quite possible to be
gloriously happy with your eyes wide open ;
they do not confuse idealism with cant.

The novelty of such an aim in fiction,
however, arises from the method of approach,
which is realism, pure and unadulterated.   The
young novelist approaches the mystery of life
with a determination, not to deduce an interpretation by deduction, through abstract the-
orising, from what we say, do, and appear ;
but to find an interpretation from observation
of what is happening within us.   She seeks to
photograph (though as an artist) the soul : to
express thought and feeling in words.   Whence
arise a new form of construction, and almost
a new style.

Almost inevitably—their heroines, seeking
below the surface—comparatively indifferent
to actual things and events, tend to egoism.
The egoist (not quite Meredith's) proves a
favourite topic.   But woman as egoist (Clare
Harthill, Zella, Nina Severing, and the rest)
is quite another creature from the complaisant

male. He, sublimely unconscious, simply assuming himself the centre of the universe, takes for granted that everything revolves about his comfort or his ambition—the world his footstool. She, consciously or unconsciously, in pride or in humility, is for ever seeking to impose herself, straining to keep in the centre, striving to dominate. She may be confident or diffident, knowing her superiority or fancying herself inferior; but she is always aware *both* of the place she occupies and the place she is determined to reach. She may dictate or dissemble, mould others or pose herself, but the aim is identical and she never loses sight of it. She may need public applause, the footlight flash, or may only care for her own good opinion ; but she is always occupied with herself. Wherefore Miss Richardson supposes that "everyone must hate to be with any other person : it was so disturbing. The disturbance of it wrung tears from her. She was seeing everyone tangled in nets . . . people being together is awful—like the creaking of furniture."

One might say, in fact, that for the most typically "new" women novelists, creation has become merged in self-expression. They write, they present life, because they must deliver their message. They offer us them-

selves, not the children of their imagination.
" I have just discovered," says Miss Richardson, "that I don't read books for the story,
but as a psychological study of the author.
. . . It was true and exciting. It meant
. . . things coming to you out of books,
people, not the people in the books, but knowing, absolutely, everything about the author
. . . they would never be stories to her.
They were people. More real than actual
people. They came nearer. In life everything
was so scrappy and mixed up. In a book the
author was there in every word."

There are two aspects of life, superficially
in direct antagonism to each other, and rather
fully illustrated by these novels, wherein we
can perhaps read "a lesson for the day."

In the first place they are, quite naturally,
much concerned with their own art. Miss
Richardson to a large extent justifies her own
methods through her heroine's comments upon
others, and Miss Mirrlees expressly states her
adherence to the opposite camp. On the other
hand, Miss Sidgwick and Miss Sinclair have
achieved remarkable success in the presentation of genius (greater than any I can recall
in English literature) : Miss Sinclair also reveals, with great intimacy, the "professionals"
of letters, and—in her remarkable " Legend "

—Miss Dane gives us another side of the same picture, while a slightly varied atmosphere hovers about "Night and Day" by Mrs. Woolf.

All these stories, inevitably, disclose the tragedies arising from a conflict between art and humanity, a man's work and his private duties or relationships—home, wife and children ; self-sacrifice and the domestic virtues.

Over against which we find ; particularly in Mrs. Mordaunt, but quite clearly also in others —Miss Macaulay, for instance, Miss Sidgwick, and Miss Sheila Kaye-Smith—a keen realisation of the complexities which arise from the different outlook of the generations, the mutual duties between parents and children, the difficulties which confront any member of a large family.

In one sense, these are two aspects of the same problem : the conflict between man as an Individual and as a social being. It appears in Shakespeare as between man, the King, or the Patriot : and man the father or husband. In George Bernard Shaw as Woman embodying Nature, the murderer of man's mind. In our new passionate assertion of individuality, the right of every woman as well as all men, for their own opinions and their own experience, in the ruthless overthrow of social con-

ventions and moral traditions, the balance
between claims certainly needs readjustment ;
and we find most of these young writers more
or less consciously concerned with the question. They see the idle error of the older
realist, who proclaimed mere anarchy and
selfish rebellion as *necessarily* right, but they
recognise much tragedy arising from what they
believe essential to individual freedom and
development. Where the home, the family,
self-sacrifice and the other Victorian ideals may
ultimately survive, we cannot perhaps yet
determine : but they have been rudely knocked
off their pedestal by a wave of youthful im-
patience and indignation which is, for the
moment, no less cruel than convention, and
satisfies neither itself nor others.

Miss Richardson, most extreme and consistent in her determination towards individuality, seems almost to ignore the problem,
not to see two sides to the question. Mrs.
Woolf remarks boldly, though incidentally,
that good work means " a power of being dis-
agreeable to one's family "; but I do not believe
that either really intends to dispose of the
difficulty so peremptorily. They are not essentially narrow in their sympathies ; and their
severe attitude should be regarded as the
record of a phase. These novels, in fact, gain

much interest and much sincerity, from their liberal interpretation of character. Without disclaiming either freewill or moral responsibility, they emphasise the need for expressing oneself without fear, the imperious demand for unchained freedom of thought ; the strength of the ego and the weakness of the herd. On the whole, I think, they suggest—what must be the final truth in the matter—that, where such claims for self conflict with claims from others, the individual must judge for himself out of his own circumstances and his own temperament. Some suffering and some sacrifice, somewhere, is unavoidable ; what in mere impulse appears as loss or sacrifice, may prove the highest gain : but dogma and formulas are always misleading and may needlessly hamper both. It is impossible to put one virtue above another, to assert that for all men at all times, it is the ultimate ideal to submit, or that one's first duty is to oneself. In the highest interests of humanity, there must be occasions for firmness in putting one's work first, there must be circumstances which compel us to deny, even our dreams. By wisely devoting their narratives to the spiritual experience of individuals, our novelists have been able to suggest a moral attitude—of strength and sympathy—which points the way for decision in each case, on

its own merits.   They illustrate the waste of
energy from interference and from regret : the
happiness and content (which mean undi-
minished vitality) that may arise from tolerance linked to faith.

Inevitably different writers have absorbed,
and expressed, the new methods in very different degrees.   Some, like Miss Sidgwick,
aim rather at efficiency and originality within
the normal.   Miss Sheila Kaye-Smith, and to
a lesser degree, Mrs. Mordaunt, frankly adopt
a masculine manner : Miss Mirrlees is historical, and Miss Fulton analytic.

Others, at least superficially, stand outside
their characters, observe and "compose"
them.   Miss Sinclair is alone in having
achieved success both in the old, and the
new, methods.

All, however, are largely influenced, if not
exclusively inspired, by what I have called
the new Realism ; the search after the new
vision—cutting away all that chokes the soul.
It is still Realism because, however impatient
of dirt and ugliness, it is directly opposed to
the Romance ideal and depends absolutely on
observation—spiritual observation—as literal
as that of the most extreme disciple of Emile
Zola.

But the realist (as Stevenson exposed him)

"doesn't see anything. . . . How can
he? His genius runs to flesh and blood, and
he hasn't room for any more of it outside his
own imagination. That's where you are with
your great realists. The visionary would have
more room. . . . He could at any rate
afford to take more risks."

Thus Miss Sinclair. In "The Legend"
Miss Dane reveals how your so-called Realist,
your writer who depicts what we call Reality,
the outward life, that is, of flesh and dirt and
misery, "is in truth a Romantic." He dare
be truthful because "its not his world." It
is "the so-called Romantic," who lives
in "this real world"; and, because he is
frightened of it, he escapes into "the world
of beauty within his own mind." So it happened in those days that Madala's first book,
written when she was young, curious, and
observant "is a shout of discovery, of young,
horrified discovery of the ugliness of life. It's
as if she said : Listen! Listen! These things
actually happen to some people. Isn't it
awful?" But in her "last book, in the pretty,
impossible romance, there you have your realist
full-fledged : shut your eyes! Come away
quickly! These things are happening to *me*."

Our Romance-realists, on the other hand,
see that "the flesh and dirt and misery" are

no more than "outward life" : and not fearing the *real* world, they seek Beauty and find
it, in a vision of the immortal soul. This is
their protest, their individuality, their sever-
ance from the herd-human, their freedom and
their independence: that—passing over the late-
Victorian sex problem-drama, leaving behind
them the grossly literal materialism of their
immediate predecessors in art, they have pene-
trated, if "through a glass darkly," into the
absolute realism that is spiritual—of the Soul,
wherein dwell Faith, Hope, and Charity.
Towards the Vision they look up and on, not
in and down.

CONTENTS

MAY SINCLAIR

SOME CONTEMPORARY NOVELISTS

MAY SINCLAIR

APART from the fact that Miss Sinclair published novels before some, at least, of her contemporaries could use the pen ; there is a certain maturity in her work which places her somewhat alone. I should attribute the sureness of touch which one also detects in Rose Macaulay to the confidence of youth, that in Ethel Sidgwick to fine literary craft, that in Sheila Kaye-Smith to a deliberately assumed costume, while Miss Sinclair's is the fruit of experience.

The others clearly are still more at the stage of experiment and one cannot be certain about their ultimate achievements.

Yet Miss Sinclair is no less vital, one might say no older than they. It is because she has kept alive and remained young, that she belongs—unmistakeably—to the new movement.

Experience only adds strength and clearness of vision to her identity with modern thought. She is concerned with what really matters to her younger contemporaries, interested in what they care most about. And she understands. Her genius for moving with the times is evidenced, incidentally, by her appreciation of Miss Richardson (the most advanced of all our novelists) quoted below. But it is equally obvious in her own work. "The Tree of Heaven," for instance, reflects the war atmosphere most poignantly from the point of view of those who were young then. "Tasker Jevons" is a genius of to-day: following, and quite a new type, the Victorian genius in "The Divine Fire." "The Creators" gives us the atmosphere of the professionals in literature—parallel with Miss Dane's "Legend"—as it was passing from one generation to the next.

It is not necessary to claim equal genius for every one of the novels : our point remains that Miss Sinclair is always contemporary, or up to date, no less in her latest work than in her earliest.

As one would expect then—from this readiness to move on and remain young—Miss Sinclair's sympathies have always embraced many issues ; though she shares with Miss Sidgwick and Miss Dane a special intimacy among the society of those who write and love books.

This is embodied, with rare skill, in that
marvellous story of "The Creators" : a
record, not of one genius, but of at least three:
other persons of the drama being almost, if not
quite, supreme—each in his or her own de-
partment. It is a unique revelation of different
artistic temperaments, all more or less suffering from private human claims and uncongenial
surroundings: building up four or five dramas
within one ; since, naturally, the problem dif-
fers for different cases. Miss Dane, with a
precisely similar atmosphere, seeks the opposite effect, by absolute concentration on one
example. In both we see that the friends of
genius are often more bitter than genius itself;
as they witness the sacrifice of fine art to
common humanity.

Miss Sinclair, however, does not attempt to
solve the problem or dogmatise upon the moral.
Her Jane Holland remains a great novelist
and, if not quite ideal as wife or mother, holds
her family's affection; giving and taking
supreme happiness from home life. Love and
art both cause pain and bring joy: if the combination involves strain, it is worth while: one
claim cannot stand, permanently, above the
other.

George Tanqueray, being a man, finds his
own problem more simple: because the masculine attitude is, naturally, more selfish.
Tradition justifies him in putting his art first:
though, paradoxically, he had appeared to risk

more by his "unsuitable marriage." Only he makes no attempt to face, or accept, the responsibilities involved. Crudely speaking, he neglects his wife (as Jane never ignored her husband) and makes no attempt to understand her emotions. It is luck, and her goodness, which more or less reconciles fate in the end: though his response is sincere.

After these, comes Nina who never hesitates. Though her friends imagine that she alone remains gladly loyal to art, rejecting all human pleasures in proud self-sacrifice; she *knows* that for her love and passion are the only real things; which she has missed because she cannot attract or inspire.

It is Owen, however,—the most conventional genius of them all; in whom the divine spark kills not only the taste for life, but even all patience with the professional machinery of art. Yet he alone finds complete happiness in marriage; simply because Laura is able to smooth the way for him by the enthusiasm of her devotion and the popularity of her "little" gift. Laura, it would seem, is the only creator whose creations please ordinary folk. Having no pride in her own talent, she yet cherishes it for the simple pleasure it affords and for its practical efficiency. She is the normal woman; bringing sunshine alike to those who know her, and those who read her. Wherefore the Vision of Owen is not lost to the world.

Where "The Creators" stands nearly alone

is in its atmosphere; which combines the soul of art with the local colour of professionalism in art.   Most writers treat these subjects apart: choosing either a genius outside the craft, or smaller men practising it with varied, but not distinguished, success.

So far as we reach any generalisation, or philosophy, on this problem, it may be found in two statements which illustrate one truth. "There are some things "—asks the average person—" I don't see how you can—without experience."

" Experience?   Experience is no good—the experience you mean—if you're an artist.   It spoils you.   It ties you hand and foot.   It perverts you, twists you, blinds you to everything but yourself.   I know women—artists— who have never got over their experience, women who'll never do anything because of it."

So it is written, on the contrary, of George Tanqueray: "He doesn't see anything "— about his wife—" How can he?   His genius runs to flesh and blood, and he hasn't room for any more of it outside his own imagination. That's where you are with your great realists."

Tanqueray himself fears at least as much danger from celebrity as from family ties—or personal experience: " Live in the country where nobody's likely to know you're celebrated till you're dead.   But if you *will* live in London, your only chance is to remain obscure.   There

are in London at this moment about one
thousand celebrated authors.   There are, I
imagine, about fifty distinct circles where they
meet.   Fifty distinct hells where they're bound
to meet each other.   Hells where they're
driven round and round, meeting each other.
Steaming hells, where they sit stewing in each
other's sweat—loathsome hells, where they
swarm and squirm and wriggle in and out of
each other.   Sanguinary, murderous hells,
where they're all tearing at each other's
throats.   How can you hope, how can you
possibly hope to do anything original, if you're
constantly breathing that atmosphere?   Hor-
rid, used-up air that authors—beasts!—have
breathed over and over and over again."
   Hence his passion for living alone and
isolated.
   In "The Divine Fire," indeed, Miss Sinclair herself has partially separated genius
from craftsmanship.   Superficially, and in his
material circumstances, Keith is influenced
by contact with editors—of very varying efficiency: even by personal experience in a
successful bookshop: but his genius is a thing
apart; scorning the easy way, hating the policy
that might secure success.   He is, in fact,
altogether a different type: embodying the
Victorian ideal of a rough-hewn poet: humbly
born, hardly nurtured; with the tiresome
nervousness of under-bred poverty, and the
sublime self-confidence of the humble egoist.

Life is not for him a conflict between realised
contradictions in duty, but a passionate problem of personal idealism.   The struggle is
always—as it were—against himself.   His
love is the crown of his genius; its inspiration
and its expression.   The plot accordingly rests
on far more dramatic foundations (which are,
again, conventional) : the clash of distinctions
in class, the acute, private, workings of a
sensitive   conscience,   the   dream   of   heroic
chivalry.   The   story,   in   fact,   approaches
romance.

" Tasker Jevons," written much later, is—
on the other hand—essentially the genius, as
he is conceived to-day—neither professional nor
remote.   His social " impossibility " is not
picturesque (like that of a romance-genius)
but aggressive and grotesque.   He is a very
much revised version of the long-haired primitive: though, indeed, he has some minor difficulties with the Queen's English and his taste
is distinctly barbaric.

Tasker,   however,   reveals   some   culture,
considerable education, and the power to shine
in society or with the elite.   His overwhelming
egoism is unexpectedly subtle: comprising a
somewhat unusual conception of morality—
towards woman, with surprising chivalry and
uncanny insight.   What baffles criticism is the
man's imagination and understanding.   He
has, in fine, a personality which (for all its
brute violence) can satisfy the woman he loves

—in the end. He irritates chiefly from an obstinate determination neither to expose, nor explain, himself. He is more complex, bigger, and on the whole more charming than the poet-bookseller; but proportionately far more difficult and more productive of tragedy. Carrying women and the world in his stride, he—too frequently—produces shipwreck.

Miss Sinclair finally startles her readers, by bringing peace and sanity out of the war.

Whence we turn, naturally, to " The Tree of Heaven." As already indicated, no national or race psychology is here attempted. The world-tragedy is used, by a great artist, as local colour for private tragedies. Nowhere else, however, can we discover so striking a proof of Miss Sinclair's unconquered vitality. Suffering everywhere is—inevitably—supreme. The noblest of parents are left bereft: youths of promise are cut off in their prime: their sister loses the lover she had just realised: the torture of a sincere conscientious objector is laid bare. Yet the impression remaining is one of beauty and happiness, faith and love. What we remember most vividly, what we recognise as the permanent gift from the whole story, is a fine picture of the splendid possibilities within humanity. Men and women are shown mighty in tribulation; as they had been glorious in joy. In part, no doubt, this effect is produced by the rare understanding between two generations, the comradeship of both Father and

Mother with children, the fine sanctity of
marriage. But, though we have doubts and
difficulties—without which life cannot be—the
best pervades all. Because there is patience
in misunderstanding, and trust under the
clouds, none of the characters prove ultimately
false to themselves. Faith is justified of her
children. It is, indeed, a glowing justification
of Man's real nature.

Once more, again, Miss Sinclair proves her
vitality, her adaptability, and her continued
youth, in "Mary Olivier," where all these
conditions are reversed. This is a profound
tragedy, the poignant record of a wasted life.
But, on the other hand, it is a successful experiment in the manner of Miss Richardson.
Of course, Miss Sinclair is too great an artist
to imitate. Superficially, she does not recall
the model. But she has here entered right
into the last stronghold of the new movement;
adopting a scheme and manner that is absolutely the same. Which is to say that this
whole, fascinating story is a record (*not* a
composed picture) of one life, the experience
of daily emotion given to one charming girl.
All the characters, all the events, each stage
of Mary's development, are drawn from within;
as they rise gradually above the horizon of
her consciousness. We have, not only her
words and deeds; but her thoughts, her emotion, her instincts—even the sub-conscious
self. The actual story, indeed, has more form

than any of Miss Richardson's—something not altogether unlike a beginning and an end; the persons and the happenings are more closely linked and dramatically arranged; but it is written with the same "final" realism, the same inward atmosphere, the same devotion to reality. Even the terrible shadow of inherited insanity, from which none of the family is quite exempt, comes to us only as its hold tightens round Mary herself. It is not implanted from without by the onlooking novelist: he who knows what the victim only suspects. It is not, perhaps, over-fanciful to find in it some justification (or explanation) of the *composed* narrative. Lives so tortured do often move in a vicious circle: and being largely cut off from humanity at large, *are* rounded off and completed after a fashion more nearly akin to fiction than to the experience of ordinary, more fortunate, individuals.

For this reason we regard Mary Olivier as of unique importance to our central argument. Because it remains, at present, the one deliberate variation (from an experienced novelist) of Miss Richardson's new methods: an indication, perhaps, of the permanent influence they may be destined to effect upon English literature.

It is not necessary to enlarge upon the art of Miss Sinclair in general terms. Its essential qualities are capability, catholic sympathy, and generous optimism. But here, and for us, its

value depends on the fact that, through main-
taining her youth, seeing and welcoming the
best in all new movements and tendencies, she
has moved with the times; so that, although
she has been writing for over twenty years,
she is yet absolutely one with the art of to-day,
a leader among war-novelists as advanced as
the most original.

AUDREY CRAVEN	1897
MR. AND MRS. NEVIL TYSON	1898
TWO SIDES OF A QUESTION	1901
DIVINE FIRE	1904
HELPMATE	1907
JUDGMENT OF EVE	1907
KITTY TAILLEUR	1908
THE CREATORS	1910
COMBINED MAZE	1913
THREE SISTERS	1914
THE TREE OF HEAVEN	1917
TASKER JEVONS	1919
MARY OLIVIER	1919

ELEANOR MORDAUNT

ELEANOR MORDAUNT

THERE is a somewhat severe aloofness and grim humour about Mrs. Mordaunt's work, which recalls—though it does not attempt—the masculine attitude of Sheila Kaye-Smith. She is, indeed, of those who stand outside their characters, dependent upon observation, and do not despise melodrama in construction. Her colouring is deep and vivid, often tragic, and always intense. She carries her people through stormy paths and paints them in sharp, firm outlines.

Mrs. Saerre (for example) in "The Pendulum" is not only Michael's mother—and one of the noblest mothers in fiction; she is also Saerre's wife, proud of her "man" while she despises him; his lover till death. We associate her in our own minds with that other wonderful mother-sketch (brooding over Miss Reeve's "Helen in Love"), almost the most bitterly drawn woman we ever knew. Mrs. Saerre, indeed, is not (superficially) either hard or bitter: but she reveals—in its most

extreme consistency—that curious pride in
humility which often characterises those who
are self-conscious about their social inferiority.
She began life as a servant; she kept herself
a working woman; she hated fiercely her
children's attempt to rise; yet, all the while,
she knew she was "different," she never for-
got that Saerre himself was a "gentleman."
It seems almost incredible, though we recognise it as true to life, that one and the same
woman could be at once so rigid and so sympathetic. She was wrapped up in Michael,
devoted to him with passionate concentration.
Yet Saerre was her "man." So it is, in
varying degrees, with all her children: since
to her, as a working woman—with a standard
far more severe than that of persons more
polished, their revolts bring, in most cases,
only disgrace on the family. They will "go
their ways"; they will not conform.

It is, however, with Michael and his obvious
"superiority" that the actual story is chiefly
concerned. As a lad, he alone could be trusted
to bring home his father from the pub. He
alone could be depended upon, in all practical,
material affairs. He cheerfully shouldered the
whole responsibility for the home. He kept
things going: looked after, so far as possible,
his brothers and sisters, managed Saerre, and
worked for his mother's comfort.

Only always, beneath that early-matured
efficiency, hovered the Dream. Even from

childhood he half-believed (as his mother would never admit she did) those tales of long-lost grandeur which Saerre poured forth in his cups. Wherefore the stern determination to " better himself "—and the others—became an obsession with him. His achievements create drama: illuminated always, in his emotions, by that most fascinating, if rather elusive, of heroines, Sally Ingram; " quite the lady," but born rebel and adventuress, far more unconcerned with superficial refinement than Mrs. Saerre, more tolerant and simple-minded, but a true woman.

It is Michael's success which actually constructs the plot. He does lift himself out of the atmosphere to which his mother so passionately believes they all really belong. In the process he becomes something of a social reformer, theoretically—though not emotionally—a champion of the underdog; here dramatically opposing the more turbulent labour-fanaticism of his young brother. He does happily marry—the lady. It is Sally, however, and not his own shrewd intellect or practical efficiency, who—ultimately—gives him the wider outlook. Without her he would be self-satisfied, self-absorbed, morbidly hostile to all mankind and the social order.

In " The Processionals," on the other hand, Mrs. Mordaunt attacks the problems of society from another standpoint. Here we discern the inadequacy of modern life for the middle classes

4

—especially those stagnating in "county" backwaters, for whom Respectability proves a hard god. It is, in this case, the father who escapes; a younger man, indeed, than any of his children; who have absolutely frozen to type. Because of their somewhat exceptional hardness, the eternal conflict between the generations assumes tragic proportions; and Hugh d'Eath's experiences, while he is supposed to be vegetating in a health resort and after the report of his death abroad, provide a fascinating record of the soul's awakening— accomplished (like that of Mrs. Heyham in "A Lady and Her Husband") after middle life. The man experiments in extremes: leaving the ordered monotony of a "county" existence, for the chaotic drama of life, as seen from the surgery of a dockyard doctor, south of the Thames. Here he renews his youth, discovers his manhood. He steps down from the shelf where he had been fixed (for good as they fancied) by the Family.

Mrs. Mordaunt has chosen, however, to close her tale with the Return of the Prodigal. As, one by one, D'Eath's energies revive, he comes to see that they merit an object: and that, after all, the care of his children remains his obvious duty. For their part, it appears life had fallen to pieces without him. Lacking a central figure, unified control, someone to sit at the head of the table ; the family became quarrelsome, torn by jealousies, ineffective and uncomfortable. Wherefore they welcome him as " the Master ": and we are left to see that, while he had learnt to play the part, they—too —were ready to fall in line.

The experiment proved a success.

In " The Park Wall," too, Mrs. Mordaunt, describes a " break with the family " : here following a line more familiar to her contemporaries. Among other points of resemblance, it is written far more from within (as a revelation or expression: not from notes observed); and it reflects life, exclusively, from the woman's vision. Alice makes her own life— not with any very conspicuous success indeed —but in courageous loyalty to her own ideal. Ultimately her vigour, and determination of purpose, also justify *her* experiment in revolt.

She had been " different " from the beginning: her family are as conventional (though in a different pigeon-hole) as the D'Eaths. They did not approve the " wild man " she accepts as husband: still less can they pardon her brave bid for liberty, the inevitable consequence of disillusion. He, indeed, savours somewhat of the Adelphi melodrama. He is startling—to modern conceptions—in his primitive, boisterous cruelty and coarseness: his stormy infidelities, childish jealousies; and sublime indifference to others. He exhibits a certain diabolical ingenuity in the plot to put her in the wrong. Such a character, such incidents, indeed, could only be tolerated in one of those unhealthy, tropical, corners of the world; to which our imperial needs have driven various types of Englishman. In practical affairs, linking science to commerce, he is both enterprising and effective, taking the long view; power and pleasure share, almost equally, his ambition.

And because, however adventurous and romantic in her private emotions, Alice found herself utterly foreign to the whole atmosphere, quite incapable of holding, or moulding, her man ; she never regretted the opportunity he, in the end, afforded her of leaving him. She persisted, moreover, in her support of the implication, (his cunning device), that her small son was illegitimate: simply to satisfy her passionate determination that he should grow up her own, hers only: knowing nothing of, owing nothing to, his hated father.

The tortures inflicted upon her by those perfect Pharisees, her " respectable " family; are drawn with spirit and vivid truth. Alice is humble and miserable, yet firm: winning peace in the end.

In " The Family " Mrs. Mordaunt seems, as it were, to collect her forces for a final and comprehensive attack on her favourite topic. I do not, of course, mean to imply that she has joined forces with the advocates of " free love," or that she even offers any criticism upon marriage.

The characters in this story all suffer in the main—from being members of a *large* family, of which the parents (as usual in modern fiction) are curiously incompetent; and without either foresight or responsibility. The mother, indeed, reveals ineffective affection; and the father has vague, good intentions. *His* efforts are hopelessly hampered by the prejudices of a country squire : who grudges the expense of keeping his children, will not spend money on properly educating them for any suitable profession, and yet furiously resents the idea of their going into trade—unless it were "beer." "To go into the church: that was a reasonable career—for a younger son—but whoever heard of anybody who was anybody being a doctor! Doctors ranked with lawyers, who were bowed to, but not invited to the house except for the discharge of their professional services. . . .

"Yet they went on having child after child, content with trimming up the cradle afresh, in pink and blue ribbons and muslin. As though human beings were always babies, could live in the cradle."

It is fairly obvious that Mrs. Hebberton would have sincerely welcomed such a solution, and the squire always persisted in regarding them as "her" children and "her" responsibility.

The tragic consequences are inevitable. One son, Sebastian, having finer feelings than

" the others," and being cursed with a modest shrinking from self-assertion, ruins his life by an indiscretion with a dairyman's daughter; and floundering heroically among the complicated consequences—following the girl's death in child-birth—ultimately loses his reason; and spends the remainder of his life like a frightened child, mothered by one of his sisters.

His brothers gradually leave home, dropping—one after the other—into different occupations: all nearly as low down, socially speaking, as could well be imagined, but not any one of them quite destructive of simple pleasures. The eldest sister marries for money, is soon—quite justifiably—divorced, and, being deserted by her lover, drifts into selfish dependence upon any of the family who are willing to lend a hand. The youngest accepts an honest, and fairly prosperous, tradesman: having started her career as " one of the young ladies " in his emporium.

There remains Pauline, the heroine, who was the first to rebel openly, " always quite sure what she wanted "; from whom one at first expects romance and adventure. But her strength of character finds other channels for exercise and, as the old people lose influence, she—in her turn—becomes the rallying point and practical centre of the family. In its more personal, and intimate, bearings, indeed, her early marriage was not a success. After the quarrel, inevitable where the two possess so little in common, and after mutual expressions of regret, the worthy clergyman " did not kiss her, simply because to his mind there was a time for everything." She could never understand his theory of " what really was ' seemly ' and what ' unseemly ' in married life. Why everything was right when her husband was in the mood for dalliance, and not at all ' nice ' when he was not."

Nevertheless, after his own fashion, the " reverend " was a good sort; and his home offered certain advantages to all the family. After his death, Pauline shouldered the whole tribe with heroic devotion; refusing, indeed, the complete co-operation of her best friend and counsellor, Edward Grice, who wanted marriage at the eleventh hour. " I've waited a long time," he pleads; and her retort is final:

" If you had loved me desperately, you would not have been content with waiting. I believe that's it. I need someone who loves me desperately. I don't want patience, or affection, or even goodness. I want something different—I don't know what ; but something that will sweep me off my feet. . . . I don't want life to be made easier. I don't think I would mind if it was made terrible—only it must be life."

Having missed her ideal, she found happiness in self sacrifice.

It is she, also, who understands what had really happened to her own people:

> " There was nothing of the country-bred family left about them : the clean candour of the eyes, the complaisance . . . the city had got them, would keep them, till they were dead and buried—in cemeteries instead of churchyards. They were just part of the dull woof and warp of city life, in which—like all course materials—a thread more or less is of little moment. They would go on getting older and older . . . it was not probable that any great tragedies or any great joys, would ever come to them. And yet all," save two, " were still under thirty."

The present generation, indeed, are more " grown-up " than their elders: " I believe *we* really belong to an era in which infancy ended with second childhood. The calm decision of the ' nursery-party,' as we used to call them, is beyond me, much as I envy it." But, " if it comes to that, we are all egotistical. The only difference is we were always wondering about ourselves, and they are always quite certain about themselves."

But Pauline has faith in " this new century ":

" It will be like a room when the doors and
windows are flung open, after ages of being shut
up, with drawn blinds. The sun and the dust
will be coming into it : the wind blowing over
the china, scattering the papers, overturning
everything—but the stuffiness will be gone.
. . . It will be a sort of spring cleaning ;
there'll be a lot of noise and bustle and turmoil."
And if, after all, " things are all put back into
the same place," they " will be fresher and
cleaner—all the better for being aired."

The philosophy, certainly, suggests both a
solution and a hope: reaching beyond the
immediate problems of this particular story.

Mrs. Mordaunt is not, I think, very successful in the short story where, indeed, women
have seldom excelled.   " Before Midnight "
is clearly intended to express that sense of
the semi-magical, some element of mystery
only occasionally realised which crosses the
paths of man, leaving him puzzled and maybe
impatient with what he cannot understand.
The topics which most of these tales touch
upon lay outside our usual experience, and
raise questions which suggest the supernatural.
But, unfortunately, they just miss conviction;
though one sees, perhaps, what the author has
in her mind; which, if successfully achieved,
would have been worth the attempt.

There are, however, one or two incidental
passages in the volume, which reveal a good
deal of Mrs. Mordaunt's general attitude to-

wards life and her work, and are, in themselves, noteworthy.

It is interesting to reflect, for example, that "I've never read anything adequate about fear. I've never heard anyone say anything that's any use about it—that gives one any idea of what it really is."

They were an unusual couple, too, who could say: "Other people love with their hearts, with their passions; but we love with a sort of hate, an incalculable, devouring curiosity."

There is great vigour of expression, in this description of a certain disreputable "crew," among whom the lost hero was found:

"It was like nothing so much as the turning up of a flat stone—a lot of weedy, white-faced decadents, stupid with absinthe."

Convention is happily summarised in the observation upon Lord Leyton's estate:

"There must be nothing left about that could offend the eye. Loose morals and loose scraps of paper alike—the great thing was that they should be out of sight."

Mrs. Mordaunt realises, indeed, the subtle ugliness of country life; and proclaims it with her accustomed vigour.

"Nothing could reconcile Margaret to all the killing which went on. To her mind the country seemed like a sort of shambles." The girl, she thought, "belonged to the country—

the lush, fertile country. And Robert, too,
he belonged to it. What wonder if they had
been caught in its seductive toils? It was
what the country was full of, seemed to be
made for; the propagation of each after its
own kind; every beast and bird, and insect and
flower, was busied over it—multiplying and
killing, that was the whole sum of country
life.''

It is one view, and a bitter one, of the
primitive: a savage denial of the idyllic.

In Mrs. Mordaunt, we cannot discern anything consciously new or ultra modern. Yet,
singularly efficient without finished artistry or
subtle psychology; she has a cool, penetrating,
gift for emotional analysis and a dramatic instinct for composition. She, too, is a dissector
of souls: and certainly not romantic. She does
not depend on *the* social problem, as it was
so fondly expounded by her immediate predecessors: but working upon some typical group
of characters who create atmosphere—reveals
the imprisoned individual, thereby crushed or,
after suffering, matured: whence comes personal drama, rather severe, perhaps, if not
actually cynical.

It is not, I think, altogether fanciful to
compare the relation between Mrs. Mordaunt
and her contemporaries; with those of the
Brontës among the women pioneers. Like
them, she is not quite in line with the main
developments of her age. She, too, has in her

a certain violence of phrase and thought, an almost savage intensity that approaches the melodramatic. Yet she assists progress. Surrounded, as we are to-day in fiction, with a rather exotic atmosphere of the fine shades drawn out by an infinity of talk, analysis, and introspection: there is certainly room for the full-blooded story of youth, not very consciously concerned about the universe.

Tragedy for her finds its justification in the shrewd comment applied to one who " was already half-consoled for all those troubles which youth is never quite happy to be without ": while for the quiet, good, girl—who suffered without protest—" what *she* needed in life; was dying for—was the lack of something, at least, of the spirit of pink roses and gay ribbons ": a little colour, a little food for the imagination.

It would appear that " if God stepped in at all, it must be merely as an umpire, to see that there was fair play." The Visionary must save his own soul.

ROSE MACAULAY

ROSE MACAULAY

WITH Miss Macaulay at her best one is captured, irresistibly, by sheer delight in good
workmanship: art, which does not, as it happens, at all depend on the special characteristics which we associate with quite modern
fiction. The distinction, in fact, touches the
heart of things: because, in her work, one is
as much, if not more, interested in individual
characters, as in thought or manner. Under
the spell of her art we forget artifice.

It is true that Miss Macaulay has a marked
style of her own: the antithesis of Miss Richardson's. Few writers, since Jane Austen,
have achieved so compact a treatment of
English: and the later novelist is the more
abrupt. The peculiarity, at its best, is most
noticeable in her introduction of a new character, whereby she conquers one of the chief
difficulties in narrative. Some introduction is
generally regarded as necessary; but a long
preliminary analysis always defeats its own
end. It bores the reader, and sacrifices the

secret of good fiction: that character should
reveal itself. All lengthy comment is a mis-
take. Miss Macaulay, however, has the gift
of an ideal hostess who, in almost an epigram,
says just what is needed to put two talkers at
ease. She accomplishes it no less skilfully for
a group of arrivals as with one visitor: "Pro-
fessor Denison was a quiet person, who said
little, but listened to his wife and children.
He had much sense of humour, and some
imagination. He was fifty-five. Mrs. Denison was a small and engaging lady, a tremen-
dous worker in good causes: she had little sense
of humour, and a vivid, if often misapplied,
imagination. She was forty-six. Her son
Arnold was tall, lean, cynical, intelligent,
edited an University magazine (the most interesting of them) was president of a conversation society, and was just going into his uncle's
publishing house. He had plenty of sense of
humour (if he had had less, he would have
bored himself to death) and an imagination
kept within due bounds. He was twenty-
three. His sister Margery was also intelligent,
but, notwithstanding this, had recently published a book of verse, some of it was not so
bad as a great many people's verse. She also
designed wallpapers, which on the whole she
did better. She had an unequal sense of
humour, keen in certain directions, blunt in
others: . . . the same description applies
to her imagination. She was twenty-two."

The assured decision of this paragraph is almost unique. It reveals personality.

Much the same may be said about her management of dialogue; which has distinguished courage.

Conducting a spirited discussion upon Women's Suffrage, for example, she introduces the disputants with stark, and surprising simplicity: "Mr. Robinson said. Benje said. Louie said. Jerry said. Cecil said. Mr. Robinson said. Louie said."

Here is a daring repudiation of the rules against repetition, of which the dramatic value is obvious. We feel at once how one after the other drops in his contribution to the controversy: the quick response, the ready tongue, the appreciation of each other's point of view. Talk reported in this manner becomes revelation of character.

Miss Macaulay, in fact, sees her people dramatically; she visualises their personality: producing its full significance in a graphic word-picture. There is no blurring nor hesitation, no fumbling after the sub-conscious. It is not, of course, that she depends only on surface values, or paints from the outside. She has plenty of penetration and much subtlety; but her mind is made up: she writes as a spectator, not identifying herself with the creatures of her imagination, trusting rather to insight than instinct. Her understanding, indeed, is as truly a question of deliberate art as the crisp narrative interpretation.

Curiously enough, her first novel, "Abbot's Verney," approaches more nearly than any of her later work to the singularities of the new method.   It is more sub-conscious and enquiring: the whole story is seen through the hero.   The characters are much given to egotism.   In Verney, indeed, the absorption in self has been forced upon him by cruel circumstances.   Between an impossible father (paid to stay, but not staying, invisible abroad), and a grandfather, rendered suspicious by pride and love, he has simply no chance for normal development.   Being, however, essentially a "white man"—of the type that builds empires : he wins through in the end.   Dramatic and vivid in all its side issues, admirably finished as are all the persons of the tale, it is a one-man, one-idea'd book: despite even the wonderful Rosamund, with her true heroism in friendship.   Here are profound psychological problems: an individual (with whom Miss Macaulay goes near to identifying herself) struggling to *be* himself— which is the modern Idealism—against most severe odds.   But it remains more drama than revelation: modern enough in setting, but a familiar type.

"The Furnace," published the same year, is more essentially typical of Miss Macaulay's own manner.   For the immortal Betty and

Tony—almost the most ideal brother and sister
in fiction—here reveal their full charm ; cun-
ningly revived (five years later) in " Views
and Vagabonds." Though themselves unique,
they belong to a class of man for whom (like
Miss Sheila Kaye-Smith) Miss Macaulay has
a pronounced weakness. They are born
tramps: joyfully irresponsible Bohemians by
instinct, and blissfully unconscious of nearly
everything we associate with Civilisation, the
Progress of Man, or social responsibilities. In
one word, they are Youth. Miss Macaulay
avoids the pitfall (in which Miss Kaye-Smith
occasionally flounders) of over-realism in detail—betraying indifference to dirt; and depends entirely for her portraiture upon the
daintiness of her somewhat whimsical imagination. This leads her, in fact, far nearer the
truth. The heroic loyalty, the perfect understanding, the power for final self-sacrifice—
which are *within* the charm, could not have
survived contact with the friends in whom they
delight, had they lacked spiritual refinement.
The tramp nature, again, (which we know so
well in William Locke) has this remarkable
psychological affinity with the faery of folk-
lore. It perishes upon its discovery that it
possesses a soul. " The Furnace " itself is
a subtle narrative of an awakening of the soul.
These two young people achieve intimacy—as
it were by accident—with a delightful family
group who might be fairly described as the

latest products of civilisation. Mutual attraction between the types is inevitable: the consequences are tragic. Because Mrs. Venables and her children are cultured and cultivated, perfectly at home with all the fine shades of art in society, yet neither conventional nor narrow-minded; they sadly disturb the serenity of the Crevequers. There hovers about them an atmosphere of something intangibly superior which at once fascinates and tortures these gay souls. Betty gradually conceives herself in some way beneath them, and Tony's perfect understanding soon teaches him the same bitter truth. They aspire where they cannot reach, even if loyalty to their whole past would suffer the change: and, since some measure of individual love has crossed the contact, impossibility compels despair.

There, for the present, Miss Macaulay is seemingly content to leave them. There is no cure but separation; and so in the after years, though no period is ever specified; we meet once more the old ''faery'' Crevequers —prominent but not central—in another tale.

Tragedy, also—and more final tragedy, pervades the most powerful of Miss Macaulay's novels—''The Valley Captives''; another dramatic picture of the understanding between a brother and sister, misunderstood of others. Fate (here embodied in a weak father) has literally imprisoned the two with his brutal and over-bearing step-children, whose one de-

light in life is to torture the sensitive Teddy,
who happens to lack physical bravery. None
of the group has any absorbing business in
life; and existence for them becomes concentrated upon Hate in a cage. Though the
sister has more character, and far greater
courage, she—too—is dragged into the conflict
through her devoted loyalty: and the end is—
inevitable—melodrama: but melodrama that is
not false to Truth. These are all real people,
for whom we are moved to intense pity.

In her second tragedy, "The Secret River,"
Miss Macaulay is not convincing. Curiously
enough the half-magic subtlety, which she
handles with rare skill as an episode or a
character-trait—has not enough hold of her to
sustain a complete story. Michael is neither
a real man nor true mystic. He fails miserably
as a lover: nor can he read rightly the tale of
the reeds—so that the cool, dim waters closed
about his body and covered him wholly.

"Views and Vagabonds," on the other
hand, brings us back—with a fresh, wholesome
wind blowing, to the full vigor of Miss
Macaulay's sprightly genius. Pleasantly
flavoured with that youthful alert dogmatism
which permits universal tolerance and incites
to endless curiosity, characterising all under-
graduates; it further demonstrates her fine
sympathy with the ideals of unconventionality.
Here, however, we find the tramp turned
preacher. Benjamin Bunter, the well-born

blacksmith, is an incurable theory-monger: he marries a working-lady just to illustrate a principle, with the natural consequences. As she put it herself, "Ben's that young and clever an' a gentleman born an' he can marry for a sort of game, but I can't. . . . I didn't want no ideas at all, I just wanted Ben." But then he is saved by friendship with the Crevequers (though calling their irresponsibility towards life a crime); and his arguments with friends more frivolous, or with those who seriously differ from him, provide a feast of humour and subtlety: clearing the atmosphere from too much cant.

"The Making of a Bigot" follows very similar lines. Eddy, the hero, carries his Cambridge universalism, indeed, into the borderland of farce. He finds good in every theory or mission, and thinks everyone delightful. Eager to help everywhere, he muddles everything.

Whence his whimsical conclusion that he might, after all, become a novelist: "That last resort of the spiritually destitute. For novels are not like life, that immeasurably important thing that has to be so sternly approached, in novels one may take as many points of view as one likes, all at the same time; instead of working for life, one may sit and survey it from all angles simultaneously. It is only when one starts walking on a road that one finds it excludes other roads."

But, after all, he discovers one truth he had somehow mysteriously overlooked: a truth which, indeed, negatives other truths: that only the fanatic can effect reform. We must choose, *and* reject, in order to get anywhere. Universal tolerance hath its charms, but doth not become the adult. Whereby, finally, is the new made Bigot " ready to work for the right things, war against the wrong." Also to win the wife (who *had* her prejudices) that he may " start betimes upon so strenuous a career."

In her two stories directly inspired by the war, Miss Macaulay covers very interesting ground. " Non-Combatants " takes a high rank among the attempts (more specialised by Miss Delafield) to produce the home-atmosphere of the disturbed period. It touches (though not so fully as the "Tree of Heaven") the pacifist conscience: it covers a great variety of temperaments—rudely awakened to new personal problems, and for the most part—furious at the appalling waste. We have, of course, the typical war-workers—men and women at least superficially content with the consciousness of something to do, well-done: a small group of artists and literary folk who nearly manage to ignore the whole immense crime: victims of shell-shock and other—skilfully individualised—men on leave: women who have lost all: and a few others, completing the sense of universality. In the centre of the picture moves Alix, the attractive heroine, who is haunted throughout by the shame that she can't be fighting: till finally convinced that if Christianity may not be doing much it is "trying to fight war, working against it in the best ways it can think of." Wherefore, she too follows her capable mother into the church.

Here we find just that bewilderment that was our actual inheritance through those fateful years: the sense that everything was the same and yet nothing was the same; the terrible feeling that we had to go on, day after day, doing little things apparently so pitifully trivial: which were yet—by some mysterious law of our nature—the things that must be done. After all, they kept life going. "What Not" scarcely maintains the same level. Here —as in the "Secret River "—Miss Macaulay builds a whole story on *one* of her special gifts: her skill in light irony; and it will not bear the load. This rather whimsical satire upon the multiplication of Government offices—one more phase of Control—or interference— misses fire. We feel little beyond the absurdity and the exaggeration.

In "Potterism," issued this Spring, Miss Macaulay has carried on what one may call her record of contemporary impressions beyond the Armistice: when "we were all spinning round and round, silly and dazed, without purpose or power, at least the only purpose in evidence was the fierce quest of enjoyment, and the only power that of successfully shirking facts. . . . And we were represented by the most comic parliament who ever sat in Westminster, upon which it would be too painful here to expatiate.

"One didn't know what had happened, or what was happening, or what was going to happen."

Superficially, that is in its local colour, this story completes "Non-Combatants" as a record of what we have all been thinking and saying about the great war, and, here again, no serious generalisations and no profound philosophy are attempted.

It is true that the principal characters are all engaged with varying degrees of intensity, in a crusade against "Potterism," which is a synonym for everything commonplace, insincere, vulgar, and artificial. The Potter Press, run parallel with the Northcliffe, by Mr. Potter, Senior, is the embodiment of imperial and capitalist cant; the novels of Leila Yorke were written "gently and unsurprisingly" by Mrs. Potter. "Quite unmarred by any spark of cleverness, flash of wit, or morbid taint of philosophy"; they treated "life and love as she believed these two things to be, and found a home in the hearts of many fellow-believers."

Clare, the eldest daughter, held the faith of her parents: Johnny and Jane (the twins) emphatically did not. And the atmosphere was an abomination to their friends: Arthur Gideon, Jew and idealist; Katherine Varick, that rarity—a real scientist, an honest thinker, and a true woman; with the high church priest and Christian, Phillip Juke.

I am disposed to think that Miss Macaulay means these things seriously: that she actually hates Potterism:

"Oh Lord, we are all Potterish," says Gideon, "every profiteer, every sentimentalist, every muddler. Every artist directly he thinks of his art as something marketable, something to bring him fame; every scientist or scholar who fakes a fact in the interest of his theory; every fool who talks through his hat without knowing; . . . every secondhand ignoramus who takes over a view or a prejudice, wholesale, without investigating the facts it's based on for himself. You find it everywhere, the taint; you can't get away from it. Except by keeping quiet and learning and wanting truth more than anything else."

That, as we have seen everywhere, is the inspiration of the new novelists : to "want truth"; they are all up against Mr. Potter.

And yet, Miss Macaulay has exercised, in its finest perfection, all her compact geniality in narration, all her laughing humour, to keep us upon the surface of things. She seems always intent upon showing us how amusing these serious young people are; without giving us a chance to pause and wonder what their poor minds are worrying about.

There is, moreover, a really remarkable result of her extraordinarily capable manner of telling a story. The actual plot is pure tragedy. Jane, because she must have a good time always, marries one of her father's most successful young editors—a complete Potterite —(with whom Clare is passionately in love); and then discovers that she really loves Arthur Gideon. Clare, in a fit of rage at the man's devoted tolerance towards her indifferent sister, pushes him down a steep flight of stairs, to his death. Jane and Gideon each think the other really committed the murder (which had been officially accepted as " misadventure ") and, almost immediately after they had discovered happiness in understanding, he is " beaten to death by white soldiery " (in Russia) "because he was, entirely in vain, defending some poor Jewish family from their wrath."

Now I like Jane Potter, and I admire Gideon: they are both real people, vital and interesting. But it is quite impossible for me to feel miserable about their misfortunes. Frankly, I cannot discover the author's secret; though I am quite sure it is *not* bad art. In Miss Sinclair's "Tree of Knowledge" one overlooked the horror through the fine faith in humanity: here one scarcely notices it through sheer joy in the brisk gaiety of the picture.

There is, indeed, something rather alarming about the ease with which Miss Macaulay now handles her material. This passage might certainly have been written by Miss Dorothy Richardson; and is far too subtly similar to be called a parody:

" That lunch at the Florence . . . my gray suédes, I had. . . . Just you and me; wouldn't it be rather nice? . . . He kept looking . . . his eyes awfully blue, with black edges to them. . . . He bought me violets, but he went to see her. . . . She gets everything, just by sitting still and not bothering. . . . College makes girls awful. . . . Pig. . . . Oh, I can't bear it. Why should I? "—and so on.

Hers, indeed, is the power of the pen: and just because her stories provide us always with such perfectly delightful company who never *intrude* their ideas, we regard most of them with a good deal of sub-conscious respect. Smiling, we do not forget.

As a whole, however, Miss Macaulay carries one with her triumphantly through the wildest of Youth's enthusiasms: largely because (as she says of her own Anne) " a sort of silent twinkling underlay even her more serious conversation." For the most part, we find ourselves in the delightful company of College friends who " always know what you mean "; who all wish " to be the sort of per-

son who ignores foolish laws "; dismissing the
more conventional as "too old to know better." Like the Rich "they love words! exalt
them, make them fulfil too high an office. How
they talk and talk, and explain and explain,
and turn everything upside down, and all
one knew so well, and words made nothing
clearer."

But she understands, also, the infinitely
simple ideal of Ben's wife: "One's got to be
pleasant, I suppose": which is expressed
briefly, because "the Poor, too, love words;
but they keep them in their proper, lowly,
place, to describe things concrete, physical,
external."

It is finally the tax-collector who has the
last word: "That's the idea"—incidentally
of Socialism, but also of novels by Rose
Macaulay—"mix us all up and prepare our
minds—till the time comes."

ABBOT'S VERNEY	- -	1906
THE FURNACE -	-	1907
THE SECRET RIVER -	-	1909
THE VALLEY CAPTIVES	-	1911
VIEWS AND VAGABONDS	-	1912
THE LEE SHORE -	-	1912
THE MAKING OF A BIGOT -		1914
THE NON-COMBATANTS	-	1916
WHAT NOT - -	-	1918

SHEILA KAYE-SMITH

SHEILA KAYE-SMITH

SUPERFICIALLY, for several reasons, Miss Kaye-Smith stands outside our group of novelists. The most significant is her masculine intellect : a feature which cuts more deeply than the mere form of such stories as the " Challenge to Sirius " and " Tamarisk Town " where (unlike all the other novels we are considering) the narrative is told exclusively from the man's outlook.

In the predominance of local colour, the dependence upon place, for example, she leaves the feminine manner. Miss Macaulay, indeed, has the academic manner and touches Cambridgeshire—but incidentally. The London of others is no more than the natural centre of intellect and society : country surroundings are merely illustrative of a character-type : Miss Sidgwick uses France and Germany to accentuate race distinctions.

Miss Kaye-Smith is mainly inspired by locality : elsewhere the stimulus came from thought and emotion. The fact indicates a deeper difference : she works from study and observation, while they depend upon experience, instinct, and emotion. In the conventional sense, therefore, she is more professional (here approaching Miss Sidgwick), not attempting the new realism; and, manlike, she leans to melodrama. It is a similar distinction to that observed between George Eliot—who took up subjects—and Fanny Burney or Jane Austen —who revealed themselves. The class of subject resembles, most obviously, Hardy's: and, in this sense, most of our contemporary novelists do not take up a subject at all—outside Life and Truth. They merely express themselves, and their point of view.

In treatment, again, she is more brutal, or masculine, than any of her contemporaries— save possibly, Mrs. Mordaunt. She spares us no details of dung and sweat from the farm-yard : being apparently convinced that the romance of the country-side needs strong meat from the realist. She is frankly rustic in speech.

It is a commonplace of social reformers that the sordidness of village life is no less repulsive than a slum-street. We have long left behind us the innocent milkmaids of the pastoral. But it is nevertheless, a matter for criticism that Miss Kaye-Smith has not quite escaped that fondness for dirt—which characterises the school : and we are haunted, at times, by the suspicion that she has " got up " her localities from books and hearsay, without having herself " lived " them. Here is a little too much " scenery " for the village drama.

I cannot, for instance, quite believe in the " Isle of Thorns," wherein the melodrama is perilous. Sally has *really* lost some of her natural instincts and inherited refinement. The adventurer, too often, descends to the level of one to the manner born. Seeking colour or romance, she loses her soul and her imagination altogether. Andy, at times, does violence to one half of his double nature; degenerating to the " impossibles ": and Raphael tolerates cheerfully what a man of his nature could, and would, have avoided. Yet the story-scheme was to glorify adventure, to idealise the born rebel, the man, or woman, who keeps a child's heart; but it just misses the poetry and the imagination (with which R. L. Stevenson has clothed the tramp)—the glow of youth, which remains beautiful—and we suspect she misses because she has studied, and not lived.

It is, perhaps, in her studies of the " old " Sussex that we should rather look for Miss Kaye-Smith's sincerity in local colour; for she is an adept (as, again, have been few women) at the historical novel. Humphrey Lyte, in the picturesque " Tramping Methodist "—of the Regency days—is a true rebel; and so, above all, is " Starbrace," that fine fool of a man, the swaggering comrade of smugglers, who would

ride away from his lady love; choosing rather
the glorious risks of free adventure in a
world of turmoil, finding his death in battle
against the Pretender at Prestonpans.

"Tamarisk Town," again, does not betray
the midnight oil. Here we have town life re-
placing the village; and—for whatever reason
—the draughtsmanship is both finer and more
assured. The book is, mainly, a study in
egoism : revealing that struggle which is the
chief mainspring of drama, between a man's
personality and his ambition, between what
himself is and the impression he longs to stamp
on the public, between his vision and his work.
It is the more subtle, and more dramatic because, in this case, we recognise Vision on both
sides of his nature. Practically, and as others
see the man, Councillor Moneypenny was an
idealist. If his outlook was parochial and his
aims paltry, they at least reveal a steady
imagination and iron will. It was he alone
who could visualise Marlingate as it might be
—a select and prosperous resort, developed
with taste, for a defined purpose, tempting the
best people: not a get-rich-quick affair, but a
sound, steadily progressive, investment. It
was he alone who had the intelligence, the far-
seeing courage, the instinct for selection, which
could clothe his ideal in bricks and mortar.
His, too, the personality to prevail over his
fellow-councillors who were at once more

cautious and (once they caught a glimmer of
his idea) more crude and impatient.

To this obsession of the solitary dreamer,
we find opposed a contrary vision :—that of
Morgan le Fay, the elfin woman : for whom the
old town, asleep in its haunting beauty, offers
a very different appeal.   She is jealous, too, of
her man's absorbing materialism, his passion
for the child of his brain.   Let him persist
at his peril.   He may build Marlingate—at the
cost of her love and his own Soul.   But she has
come too late, he has plotted and planned too
long.   When behold (as she had warned him)
there slips into his heart a full realisation of
what his choice meant, the thwarted egoist
turns furiously upon himself ; once more rousing the full force of his immense will-power—
now turned demoniac—to the destruction of all
he had wrought in his pride.

Marrying carelessly—in all the bitterness of
a dead soul—his solitary old age is yet further
tortured by witnessing a repetition of the same
struggle in his only son.   The boy, having inherited the old man's first enthusiasms, is left
in the dark before the stern destructiveness of
the new policy.   He, too, loves Marlingate ;
and to him also, comes the love of a maiden
—for whom the town of his dreams has no
inward significance.   Reversing, as we feel
inevitably, his father's decision, he finds new
happiness in wider fields: breaking the chains
implanted by childhood memories ; winning at

once the freedom of his own soul and the reward of unselfish love.   He is the smaller
egoist, and the bigger man.

Here we see Miss Kaye-Smith at work upon
a slight variant of the theme that inspired
(three years before) her almost epic " Sussex
Gorse "; where, again, Reuben Backfield loses
everything for fierce love of the Boarzell acres
—the savage common of gorse and furze, of
marl and shards :—

" It lay in a great hush, a great solitude, a
quiet beast of power and mystery.   It seemed
to call to him through the twilight like a love
forsaken.   There it lay: Boarzell—strong,
beautiful, desired, untamed, still his hope, still
his battle."

In the mad frenzy of possession, he is sus-
tained through seventy years of desperate
fighting; careless even of human sacrifice,
losing almost without a pang, every man and
woman linked to him by natural affection.
Gone from him were his brother Harry, his two
wives, his six sons, and his two daughters;
gone, too, others with whom the human bond of
love was yet closer.   Yet he must fight on.

Here is the true passion for Mother Earth
(as she has hinted it, also, in " Spell Land ");
if it be fiercely consecrated to one tiny spot
thereon.   Such is the sacrifice that our gods
demand.

It is, however, the " Challenge to Sirius "
which is most typical of Miss Kaye-Smith at

her best: at once most completely masculine
and most sincere. There is a sentence, which
reveals its essential philosophy, to be found in
Mrs. Mordaunt's " The Pendulum "; curiously
enough, recalling the significant appeal to
loyalty in women which Anne Elliott so
eloquently expressed in " Persuasion ":—
" People so often wonder why a man is not
faithful to a woman for whom he undoubtedly
cares; and yet it seems that an affection like
this produces its own vacuum—a vacuum ready
to be filled for the most part, by the antithesis
of its former occupant. Or, again, he is like a
man but partially recovered from a bad illness,
sensitive, liable to catch another." So, too,
does Miss Sidgwick, pleading Romeo's Rosa-
lind for justification, suffer the, temporary,
quite honest infatuation of Charles Shovell for
Alice Eccles—*after* the first awakening of his
devotion to Violet Ashwin.

Miss Kaye-Smith, indeed, permits her Frank
two infidelities. In the first case, the digression
is little more than episode, the first stirring of
youth's young blood, wholly physical, and
without any lasting effect on character: the
almost inevitable consequence of an untutored
lad from the country being tossed suddenly
into the very centre of an ill-regulated London
circle of Bohemian failures in life: men and
women with no higher ambition among them
than " defying the law because it *was* a law ";
prompted in all their talk and action, by an un-

reasoning hostility to convention and morality.

But, on the other hand, we find real romance and manly passion combined in the love of his manhood; Lovena, the fair American—a true woman and, for at least much of his character, a true mate. Experience here elevates Frank instead of degrading him : it is not infatuation, but inspiration.

Wherefore the final return, nearing the end of life, to the familiar nature atmosphere of boyhood ; the final marriage with the sweetly simple-minded and primitive woman to whom he had given his child's heart; assumes for us the significance of a symbol. Maggie, in fact, is a true child of nature, the very spirit of Country Life : with all its dumb fancies and brooding imaginations, linked to a shrewd, elementary, materialism. Whence we see in Frank's delayed loyalty to her, that strange return to the atmosphere of our childhood, its tastes, its instincts, and its dreamings; which lies at the root of character, and, not infrequently, brings with it the highest happiness and content.

Finally, Miss Kaye-Smith has captured a similar truth in her tragic war-novel, " Little England," where the world's upheaval is used, with dramatic concentration, for the revealing of the rustic; with his sternly limited imagination, his slow but single-minded determination, and his inarticulate pathos. In the two young men (one a plain hero, the other a coward and

failure) who go to the front : in the brother who
manfully shoulders the whole responsibility of
the old farm, breaking up new land to feed the
nation; or in the sister whose crude love story
is so curiously complicated by khaki inroads;
Miss Kaye-Smith has skilfully linked the permanent in life and nature to what was, tem-
porarily, engraved thereon by the catastrophe.
However much (and there was far more in
villages than in town life), went on normally,
however often men and women loved, married,
or died, were faithful or faithless; the surface
was changed, and the depths were stirred. She
does not attempt, here, any psychological
analysis : she does not discuss social, or international, policy : but she does use, legitimately
and dramatically, the conditions which were
disturbing the whole world. It is a fragment
of genuine human history, a record of great
artistic value; which could only have been seen
and drawn by one who was very much alive at
that particular period.

Thus we find that Miss Kaye-Smith (at her
best) uses her own—more conventional—
methods of observation towards the inner
vision with which women are mainly concerned.
If far more realistic—in the old sense—than
most, she is still a realist. What we find new
in contemporary fiction, indeed, cannot be
destined to cover the whole field, to be adopted
by all. Like other genuine forward movements, it will leaven the lump, influencing, no

doubt, those who do not fall in line, those—
even—who, as a matter of judgment, are
hostile.

On the other hand, we do not expect many
women-writers to follow Miss Kaye-Smith.
She is too masculine: but as there is nothing in
her work which counters the most characteris-
tically feminine ideals ; there is, also, a certain
passionate sympathy and tenderness, which the
men of her school seldom, if ever, attain.

Sussex remains, as it were, her private park.
She has caught that mysterious personality
which does, in fact, distinguish the folk and
atmosphere of one English county from life
spent over the boundary. Probably we can all
recognise the man from Manchester, or the
Cornish man ; but a far subtler instinct becomes
necessary for differentiation between counties
that are adjacent; members of one group.
There are groups within groups : one town
on the East Coast differeth from another. And
in Miss Kaye-Smith we recognise that inner
vision, that imaginative sympathy (perfected
by Thomas Hardy) which has grown into one
particular corner of our Mother Earth. Here,
inevitably, we find silent kinship with nature,
and an understanding of primitive man : which
is the inheritance of those not caught in the
whirl of progress, not limited by London life.
Miss Kaye-Smith, obviously, knows something
—it may be much—about the " new " theories
of art and morality, on which the intellectuals

of an over-cultivated society are always busy-
ing themselves : but she has chosen to leave
such matters alone.   For her the Vision of
youth trembles under the firmament, sunny or
clouded, among the green fields or the golden
crops.   Always it savours of the soil.   Whence
her message : and that, too, has its meaning—
towards the discovery of Truth—for the most
sophisticated of us.   The background remains
eternal.

TRAMPING METHODIST	-	-	1908
STARBRACE	-	-	1909
SPELL LAND	-	-	1910
ISLE OF THORNS	-	-	1913
THREE AGAINST THE WORLD	-		1914
SUSSEX GORSE			1916
CHALLENGE TO SIRIUS	-	-	1917
LITTLE ENGLAND	-	-	1918

ETHEL SIDGWICK

ETHEL SIDGWICK

Miss Sidgwick, like Miss Macaulay, derives
the sense of efficiency which is, perhaps, the
most striking feature of her work; from an
artistic finish which is similar, and yet essentially different. There is—in the same way—no
slurring or hesitation about her work. But
what the other acquires by decisive compact-
ness, she produces by elaborate detail, and extreme literary deftness : an infinite series of
impressions or hints—firmly outlined but all in
miniature. She never indulges in broad or
dramatic effects. One might say that where
Miss Macaulay offers conclusions, Miss Sidgwick gives evidence. The distinction recalls a
description of one of her favourite heroines :
"Violet was quite impossible and only to be met
with in books—she spoke in print and moved in
half-tone pictures. She was a perfect natural
refreshment from the obvious 'vital' girl imposed by the age. She was civilised, sophisticated, attenuated, new to art. She was her own
discovery, re-discovery rather. She must have

locked herself up in the back of the book-shelves.'' It is said too of her father: '' He be-gan to listen by degrees—to the sense, that is: he loved the manner and the phrasing so much.'' The sense of literature permeates every story. All her characters '' talk in print.'' They are essentially true to nature, real flesh and blood : but a trifle over-civilised, finished to a fine ex-cess, and somewhat elusive. Their talk is too clever for real life; which may be the explana-tion of some hostility towards Miss Sidgwick, which one learns from the most earnest youth. Style and polish are more in evidence with her than either thought or emotion. Only the humour seems almost identical : or rather, per-haps, as Miss Sidgwick herself expresses it: '' Their genius is not that of humour, but comedy which is a far broader and more benevolent thing.''

There is, too, another significance about this excess of literature in Miss Sidgwick; since it specifically limits the variety of experiments : keeping her to one type, almost one group of characters. It is actually the fact that in four novels, '' Hatchways,'' '' A Lady of Leisure,'' '' Duke Jones,'' and '' The Accolade,'' different members of one family play the chief parts—at least, one individual being common to all : whereas '' Succession '' is a definite sequel to '' A Promise.''

It is, moreover, in these two groups that we find Miss Sidgwick at her best. Several

writers have at different times been acclaimed
supreme in the interpretation of genius—always
a fascinating experiment—but few, if any, can
have actually excelled the full length portrait
of Antoine Lemaure which occupies these two
long stories without a moment of dullness.
The achievement—though, naturally, allied to
the presentation of an artistic temperament—
covers separate ground; and demands a rare
combination of insight and imagination.
Somerset Maugham (in " The Moon and Six-
pence ") has accentuated its possibilities of re-
pulsiveness : Miss Sidgwick (like May Sinclair
in " The Divine Fire " and " Tasker Jevons ")
reveals its peculiar charm—the personal mag-
netism which may accompany a supreme gift

Antoine is not only attractive, but actually
loveable : partly, I think, because he remains a
child to the end. Yet the character is quite
developed : changing little, indeed, with
growth.

He is not the common type : a fine soul fixed
in glorious isolation. His family (which is
French) exist, as it were, for his perfection : all
musicians to their finger-tips. The grandfather
of the story was a composer of some note in his
own generation and a violinist of distinction,
famous in all the capitals of Europe. " Uncle "
Lucien knows the subject and is a first-class
teacher : incidentally an idolator of the traditions of the family. Antoine's mother, again,
had a soul for music : but was too wayward and

temperamental for actual greatness : more or less making a failure of her appearances in public. She marries—quite happily—a typical Englishman, an Empire-builder, who is *also* a really genial companion with exceptional understanding of the fine shades.

It is round their second son, Antoine, that the two novels centre. Revealing from babyhood an abnormal, and dangerous, sensitiveness to his mother's piano-playing, the child is soon found to have genius as a violinist; and, with the impulsiveness of their race, all the family immediately determine that he shall carry on the great name; even to further heights than were ever attained by the original Master—Lemaure grandpère. Literally everything is subordinated to this one aim ; save for the slight distractions involved in his father's demand for a short experience of life in England and a boarding-school—where he suffers a good deal from his originality and general " queerness." Otherwise the child is treasured, guarded, and trained—with severity—for the honour of the name.

Beneath this admirably organised campaign, however, Antoine's nature and character develop—not quite as they all suppose or desire. They picture him as a great performer, and he lends himself to their ambition. Here, indeed, he can satisfy the most exacting demands : because he is, actually, an executive genius; a prodigy on the platform, rousing the wildest enthusiasm in London, in Paris, and in Berlin.

But, though his nerves constantly produce the most exasperating disappointments and the affectionate alarm of those who love him; the key to his personality is unselfishness and a desire to please. Always and everywhere, we discover gradually, by the most subtle revelations of thought, word and act, that, in reality, (despite their untiring solicitude) it is they who lean upon him, not he on them. And, understanding, he long suppresses, and always curtails, the expression of his real self, which is the composer. Only by working far into the night, or hours before others have left their pillows, can he contrive, between strenuous hours of practice with Lucien, and the social duties of a public favourite—to write at all; and he is continually breaking down under the strain. The truth only becomes public property at the close of the second novel : and *then* chiefly because his grandfather's death frees Antoine from the pain of exposing how far he had moved from the old man's theories of art.

Nor does this absorbing main topic cover the whole ground. With Antoine it is only on the surface—in the accidents of daily life—that his genius disturbs his balance or sense of proportion. His intimate personal relations, his private conduct and affections, are not only expressed with engaging courtesy and candour, but governed ultimately by a determination in unselfishness and a loyalty to the ideal, which

commands our unqualified admiration. It is a
very unusual conception of genius; but the
more attractive and intriguing.

Finally, the colouring of the stories is enriched by Miss Sidgwick's quick sympathy
with the inner workings of national character
(Antoine himself being of mixed race): in
sharp contrast to the second group, which is
exclusively English.

Here Voilet Shovell (née Ashwin), though
not mechanically central throughout, permeates
nearly as much as the boy composer. In
" Hatchways," indeed, her appearance as a
charming child, is only flitting, though individual: " A Lady of Desire " records her
wooing, " Duke Jones " her honeymoon, and
" Accolade " her fine sympathy with somewhat
younger members of her own generation—
cousins and friends.

That heartless and " complete egoist " Mrs.
Ashwin appreciated her daughter (when not
disturbed by jealousy) as one " who generally
looked nice in the right places ": more en-
thusiastic observers would have called her a
fascinating beauty. We have seen, already,
that she was a perfect product of that super-
civilised atmosphere: where the best society
and the highest culture meet in an easy brilliance that transforms life into a fine art. Only
in her, Art has absolutely no hint of artifice.
Hers are a strong, sincere personality; a
vigorous intellect; and a warm heart. By

training and instinct, she contrives to be daring
in unconventionality and glorious in impulse,
while remaining the great lady and even the
wit.

She seizes both joy and sorrow with both
hands: through the crises of life proving herself
sublime and heroic in self-sacrifice. Her acceptance of full responsibility (not actually her
own) for the tragedy of a girl friend, leads to
the death of her own child and nearly her own.
There is, neither here nor elsewhere, any
shirking of deep emotion or moral values.
Incidentally also she reveals rare efficiency in
all practical affairs.

The character creates and dominates a
fascinating atmosphere : where, for all her
polish and fluency, Miss Sidgwick never deserts
reality or truth. Nor are the other characters
anyway commonplace. Of Charles, her husband, Violet says truly when he has stopped
being a baby, he will become a delightful old
man. " Nothing between? " said the Rector.
" Nothing, I fear—a first and second childhood, that's all."

The remark, however, applies only to his
character and emotions. He is quite reliable
and mature in material concerns; and, intellectually, her match. Altogether a delightful
creature; with an essential modesty that does
not prevent him from acting—when needed—
with decision and authority.

There are points of resemblance again

between him and John Ingestre—Violet's cousin, and hero of " Accolade," whose tragedy arises from the discovery of his ideal (rather an immature but a fascinating young person who worships him) some years after his marriage; since his heart had remained many years younger than his wife's. Iveagh Suir, the hero of the " Hatchways," finds happiness out of the reverse process, the unfruitful passion, not returned, here preceding marriage; though in the beginning, its failure came near to wrecking his life. There is kinship between the two younger sons, with their county families; wherein friends and relatives are, some of them tyrannical in their proud distrust of originality, others beautifully sympathetic. " Hatchways," perhaps, is a stronger story in its main plot; but rather weaker in the side issues.

" Duke Jones," wherein Charles and Violet reach their highest stage of interest, introduces a new element in its hero, the only " commonplace " figure in Miss Sidgwick's portrait gallery. The art, certainly, is *not* commonplace; but he is deliberately presented as the ordinary middle-class type of Englishman; quite innocent of the fine shades, without any experience of Society or the Intellectuals, scarcely sensitive to art. Yet the man has nobility. He is absolutely dominated by chivalry—a Round-Table knight : Violet Shovell his chosen lady. With devotion and loyalty, disturbed but not diverted by what he fancies indifference in her husband. he shoulders every available opportunity of easing her pain and anxiety, making life for her bright and easy. Wherefore, he takes up the sad case of cousin Lisette, a girl fated to vex her friends, always in trouble, more or less of her own making, and reckless of consequences. Jones is quiet, effective, and tireless in good work. He traces her, after infinite pains and with considerable ingenuity, brings her back to her friends : and finally, seeing no other way, makes the supreme sacrifice by marrying her, *and* proving a good husband : acting as father to her child. After all, he is a true gentleman and, through sheer rectitude and humility a fine conscience; rises to heroism. It is an interesting study.

The essence of Miss Sidgwick is her instinct for Literature. Sometimes, like her own Charles, " she teases the language, and fidgets her phrases : but her aim is precise in general, and her taste pure." Our appreciation depends on a quick intellect, familiarity with art atmosphere and book language, a love of the fine shades. In structure and style she is not realistic; she frankly composes; yet, in her own way, lays bare the soul. She is modern : because she does not concern herself with single emotions, whole characters, a crude clash of black and white. She is never melodramatic. Nor does the narrative make up one centralised plot. It grows out of the immense complexi-

ties and interchange which super-civilisation
imposes on human-nature. The persons of the
drama are pulled in a thousand different directions, by circumstances, place, and standards;
growing out of intellectual activity, a cultured
outlook, inherited standards. They are in
touch with that new morality which our ances-
tors would have dismissed as a perverse confusion between right and wrong, a curious twist-
ing of emotion, and a conception, rather morbid, if not decadent, of human nature. Over
the brilliant surface Miss Sidgwick moves with
ease and precision : manipulating her high-
spirited team with a cool, strong hand : drawing the picture in firm, fine, lines : never losing
our attention, or ceasing to charm. Beneath
the surface lurks Truth : real emotion, and
vivid humanity.

It is supreme art, admirably controlled.

PROMISE	-	-	1910
HERSELF	-	-	1912
LE GENTLEMAN	-	-	1912
SUCCESSION	-	-	1913
A LADY OF LEISURE	-	-	1914
DUKE JONES	-	-	1914
ACCOLADE	-	-	1915
HATCHWAYS	-	-	1916
JAMESIE	-	-	1918

AMBER REEVES

AMBER REEVES

THOUGH the silence of Miss Reeves has been unbroken for some years, she belongs essentially to the new school of novelists, if only for something typically modern in temperament— her own and her characters.

"Helen in Love," for example, is an egoist, closely allied to Miss Delafield's Zella, and only to-day would it have been possible to present a heroine so frankly in search of emotional experience. The crudities of her initial adventure, copied deliberately from the vulgar beach flappers of Beacham does not differ in essence from the subtle experiments of her developed maturity, when she adapted herself to the atmosphere of refinement. On the other hand, the direct inspiration of that first attempt is an original conception, and might fairly be called "the last word" in modernity. Helen is sister to most heroines in her sufferings from an inferior, unimaginative, family: but, seeing no way to rise, scorning despair and its resultant inactivity, she stoops to conquer. Clearly " common " people, she observes, not hampered by narrow ambitions towards respectability, can find manifold opportunities to enjoy life. Evidently they gain something, outside her experience, which they consider worth gaining, from the " boys " they annex so gaily and easily. It is not, indeed, quite clear whether Helen's comparative failure in imitation, the distaste she reveals for the kiss-casual, arises from her innate superiority, or merely proves that she was not quite sincere. It is a commonplace in human psychology that happiness we plan, and manœuvre for, has little flavour, a studied attitude generally misses its mark. For all the fever of her desires, Helen probably did not quite play up to the part. The performance was rather lacking in spontaneity and abandon.

The more subtle, and equally studied, experiments of later life; are more successful : mainly because her training for comradeship with higher-class men had been more complete : aided by friends and circumstances, not (like the other) evolved suddenly out of her own secret impulses. They do not, however, reveal any real development of character. They still indicate only the search (or what Bernard Shaw calls the instinct of the huntress) : they are still experimental : still culminate in the kiss.

So analysed we admit that Miss Reeves' heroine can scarcely appear attractive, if you

are not actually repulsed by the unhealthy pre-
occupations of her mind.   The fact that she
remains charming surely testifies to the author's
peculiar skill.

There is, in fact, a strange innocence about
Helen, a childlike naïveté in her enthusiasm
for " new " people, a delicacy in her conduct
of a flirtation; which, if not precisely pure, is
at least maidenly.   Moreover, her first (and her
last) early experiment on the Beach—which
did not in fact conform to the models inspiring
it—had a certain queer simple sincerity, and
coloured her whole life.   At the back of her
mind, Helen was always faithful to her first
love : and when, after various emotional dis-
turbances, they met again, she found that he,
too, remembered, and their quite normal wooing and marriage closes the tale.

Miss Reeves, moreover, reveals her power in
the dramatic creation of a lower middle-class
atmosphere, gradually adapted to higher
things : and even more emphatically, in some
of her minor characters.   Helen's remarkable
mother (who stands worthily beside that great
" mother " in Mrs. Mordaunt's " The Pendulum ") is a unique figure.   Her strangely
conceived passion for *making* herself disagree-
able to her own family, her deliberately
assumed cold severity, covers a nature not only
of strength, but, as kindlier circumstances reveal, of some sweetness.   The later developments of her character, under the sun of pros-

perity and success, are as attractive as they are
unexpected.

" The Reward of Virtue " follows rather
similar lines, less elaborately worked out.
Here, too, the heroine, spurred by hostility to
the conventional atmosphere of home life, is—
less adventurously—out for emotion. She, too,
starts among rather vulgar surroundings; but
is violently detached from these by an intellectual talker who, to her innocence, appears
compact of ideals, and almost a genius. She
was always, more or less consciously, " up
against " the " official explanation of love,
implied though never expressed," the parents'
idea of how a " nice girl " would behave and
feel towards her husband. So far, however,
she is not really much interested in the young
men, but in her own sensations.

Wearying somewhat of this limited field for
thought, she accepts (almost by accident) the
persistent lover—by name Day—because,
when he had fallen at her feet on the sands,
she instinctively picked him up and kissed him.
She supposed that settled it.

The change from home proves welcome;
but " she liked being alone and deciding things
for herself "; and so is rather dismayed by the
" unexpected importance of her husband.
She had not realised how much she would see
of him, or that she wouldn't be able to get away
from him, even when his temper was bad.
Fortunately, that did not often happen."

In some moods, however, she rather admires
his ruthlessness, enjoying her own submission;
though seriously annoyed to find that cheques
are not so easy as kisses to gain by submission.

Later she finds religion (as it had been
already awakened in girlhood); and when her
father's death makes her a wealthy woman,
determines to embark on good works, without
any regard to her husband's comfort or wishes.
" You can't expect me to go on always thinking
about being married when being a wife has
turned out so badly. A fine home! that I'm
never happy unless I'm out of it."

However, the social workers she had
arranged to patronise and endow, proved rather
ungrateful : a child is born, and " after all she
belonged to it, it's father couldn't alter that."
Wherefore she admits that if you stick to your
home, things will come right. " I think marriage itself has a strengthening effect on character . . . after the first year or two a married woman's happiness lies in her own hands
—only she must not expect too much—most
young girls are so romantic."

And she ends in repeating the exact words
with which, had she only known it, her mother
had heralded her own first appearance. " I
mean to be baby's *greatest* friend. . . .
I'm glad it's a girl. . . . I shouldn't know
what to do with a boy—girls are so much
easier."

A conclusion suggesting that, after all,

heroines are very much like other people, and
may even be rather stupid. In both these
stories, as in Miss Richardson, we see life
through the eyes of a young girl : finding it not
unpleasant.

" A Lady and Her Husband " breaks new
ground. It is a record (drawn in the main by
the observer) of certain rather unusual consequences of the freedom acquired by women :
an analysis of its effect on a simple-minded
middle-aged lady, who had been married for
twenty years, and was happy in her home life.
Here the progressive daughter, fearing her
marriage will leave her mother unoccupied,
and too much alone, hits on the ingenious device of educating her in social conditions,
opening her eyes to the cruel slavery of girlhood—particularly in the multiple tea-shops
from which the family wealth is derived.

Despite her surface Victorianism, Mrs.
Heyham proves both adaptable and energetic;
rather disturbing, in fact, to her husband's
most positive convictions, as to the " sheltered
life " proper to women. Developments along
this line, however, are rudely shattered by the
discovery that her husband had been unfaithful
to her—after the easy-going fashion perfectly
natural to his type, and the story closes upon
her courage in facing the personal tragedy. It
would, I think, have been more interesting, and
certainly more original, had Miss Reeves
worked out a genuine and broad-minded rela-

tionship between husband and wife (as an
achievement of middle age) merely upon her
newly found sense of citizenship, her more
active partnership in his affairs.   This is
achieved—in a measure : but would be far
more convincing without the personal tragedy.

On the whole, however, we may fairly
describe Miss Reeves as a sex-explorer : yet
she betrays neither coarseness nor prudery.
She is, after all, concerned—like the roman-
cists—with a girl's young dream : carrying into
modern conditions, expressing for the new
woman, the truth for which Jane Austen once
claimed a daring that was "all her own," (and
which actually was among the most important
of the revelations accorded us by the pioneer
women in fiction), that girls do often fall in love
before men; and, at any rate, are nearly always
quite as much interested in, and concerned
with, the subject, as their big brothers.   In fact,
they no longer accept, in this matter, the masculine ruling.   And the heroines of Miss
Reeves are quite ordinary young people; not
essentially rebels, very imperfectly well-read.

VIOLA MEYNELL

VIOLA MEYNELL

It has been well said that "Miss Sidgwick
and Miss Meynell provide a remarkable contrast. . . . Miss Meynell is astonished
afresh at each new book of hers, at each new
person she meets and introduces to us. She
writes emotionally when Miss Sidgwick writes
intellectually—and though each will use in-
sinuation rather than statement—there is a
world of difference between an insinuated
syllogism and in insinuated tear. Miss Sidgwick's method is at times obscure, but her
thought is clear : Miss Meynell's method is
clear, but her thought is obscure. Her people
move in a world where judgment is thought
abrupt and decision rather vulgar, and the
lines between ' might ' and ' might not ' are
fanciful lines."

In fact, Miss Meynell's naïveté is phe-
nomenal; and few writers reveal a more
marked individuality. Her outlook is always
that of a wondering child; absorbed and delighted by the puzzle of experience. Her

characters do not resemble Life; because they are all obsessed by one idea. Yet they are quite human : their attitude *towards* that idea is perfectly natural.

All her novels, like those of Miss Reeves, are wrapped up in one mood or group of moods—those produced by falling in love, wondering whether one is in love, or falling out again. Her heroines, too, are peculiarly simple-minded, absolutely clean in thought, inexperienced, a little Victorian. But they are, essentially, less modern than the others, and more spontaneous. They do not, like them, go out in search of emotional experience : they give themselves up more completely to whatever experience life—and a man—may bring. Yet there is no violence in passion, no abandonment to sensual impressions; the physical aspects of sex are not intruded.

It would, indeed, be impossible to express with more naïveté and discretion—one might almost say more childishly—than in the following passage, a truth on which more conventional, and analytical, realists base so much of their so-called truthfulness to life; their contention that women are equally influenced with men by a sense of sex :—

" Many of the girls were in that excited and half-sensuous mood so common to parties, when each one feels that she more than the rest has the essential power to attract, and that in every man there must be a hidden conscious-

ness of that, which might at any moment betray itself. In some this was so strong that
even if a man were known to belong to
another, that did not prevent the presumption
that he had at any rate the will to be faithless
in his admiration, though perhaps not the possi-
bility of showing his state of mind. For in
that weak mood they were mistaking willing-
ness to yield to sensation for attractiveness.
And though a girl even in the power of that
insidious social excitement might remember
with misgiving: ' but I am not beautiful,' she
could reply to herself, with perfectly satisfied
reassurance: ' No; *but I am I.*' ''

How carefully Miss Meynell has discovered
for herself what the realists have always
assumed everyone knew, though they would
not admit: how quaintly she attributes such
" naughtiness " to the " excitement " of a
" party."

Her heroines, indeed, are rather given to the
" door-mat " attitude of Charlotte Brönté,
though towards a different ideal of man.

Jennifer's state of mind was " a girl's fear of
living . . .   there was a thing which she
had long ago called ' something strange in
men,' and into this category she put occasional
incidents, not thinking or enquiring." Afterwards " her mind was in that state of devotion
to one man when other men's qualities seemed
not quite credible or entirely without the
power to interest or appeal." . . . " ' It's

wonderful what just holding his hand does for
me,' she thought, ' suddenly peace comes, absolute peace, after all those days.' ''   Dixon
Parish, the egotist, knew that '' something in
him wanted her, and something in him didn't
want her, and he just indulged both.   And
when the ' second ' something determined him
to leave her, ' she longed for the final complete
despair . . . now instinctively she grasped
at it all, *so that there could be nothing left.*' ''

You will guess that there was '' another
lady '' : '' that little process of thought and
action and habit which was called Lily Peak,
which fulfilled itself exactly as circumstances
suggested, never knocking in collision against
anything that came, but moulding itself easily
and impressionably to whatever chance befel—
that poor drifting process , which was Lily
Peak.''

Having given up Jennifer, '' he thought of
Lily as the lost, missed object of his life.   Discovery of himself was not much more than the
discovery that to love and guard and cherish
Lily was what God had expected of him.   He
found in himself all God's careful preparations to that end.   The instinct to protect someone in need of protection was so vital a part of
him that even in the midst of his passion it had
made itself felt, keeping something of him free
from Jennifer.''

The conclusion, itself, was comforting to his
masculine complacency : since whatever suffer-

ing his vacillations may cause the objects of his attention—" he always had a strange power of avoiding thoughts that would be cruel to himself. What most people must from time to time give their minds up to—regret, probing, speculation, wonder—Dixon had all his life simply shunned. His brain was very much his servant, it was his strange prevailing characteristic that his brain only thought what he wanted it to think. He did not therefore have any profitless regrets . . . he only had those which would actually be of use in influencing his actions, in making him do what he wanted to do. It was a fine economy which all his life he had instinctively practised. His emotions never flew wide of a mark; they were always what could be fitted and satisfied with the result."

Does Miss Meynell, I wonder, quite realise the fine sarcasm in this subtle analysis of the male mind?

Here, in " Columbine," Miss Meynell has revealed a man wanting two women, alternately between the peculiar attraction which each offers. " Modern Lovers " discloses one woman, differently in love with two men : a position the Victorians would have certainly regarded as indelicate. It is impossible to avoid such reflections in considering these novels; because, for all her directness of statement, Miss Meynell reveals everywhere a curious strain of ultra-feminine innocence which recalls our mothers. Nevertheless, the fact, which one is tempted (in this atmosphere) to call ugly, remains dominating, that Effie does love both Clive and Oliver. She is, literally, absorbed in each. In their different ways, governed by mood or circumstance, each seems to her the most perfect creature in the world, most wonderful of all men, creating a radiant satisfaction in her heart. Towards both she feels and exhibits " extraordinary tenderness." In her mind, there is absolutely nothing to put one above the other. The two emotions appear to be literally identical. She is, naturally, aware of the difficulties which must ultimately arise from the position. It is not, indeed, always easy to arrange her life, so as to secure both at the same time. But she achieves this, even after she is found out.

And, most marvellous of all, the apparently insoluble problem remains unsolved. That is to say, she never discovers, and certainly the reader has no clue for judgment, whether she could ever have chosen finally between them, or which she would choose. Oliver is killed, maybe he chose death, her grief was " true and sedate and decent ": but she is content with Clive. In addition to her wilful exaggeration of sentiment, Effie is strangely unguarded and over-demonstrative in manner. Describing the two sisters of this story, Clive begs his mother to " notice their curious distinct little ways. . . . For instance, Milly, you know if she has any-

thing clever or amusing to say, wilfully
deadens the voice in which she says it; she
scorns to let her voice and manner help her.
Well, now Effie is so engrossed in her manner,
and expresses herself so much by it, that her
actual words are often quite unimportant, and
even incoherent."

In the beginning, Clive had loved Milly and
she him; with an intense mutual devotion. But
Effie has no self-restraint. She is far too intense to think of others : and Clive was a man
of " conspicuous and quick attractions. . . .
His history is a history of being loved—which
might become almost tiresome in its sentiment.
For he was a great man . . . what made
the deepest impression was the long, fearless,
shy look in his eyes, which seemed both to
question you and promise you. He made an
enquiry and a pledge with his eyes, to which
you suddenly felt yourself responding uncon-
ditionally in your heart . . . he could not
help liking to talk about himself, because the
atmosphere was one of intense praise and worship. It was a subject which always went well."

Miss Meynell evades no detail of the two
sisters' adoration of her hero (nor of Effie's
tenderness towards his rival). Thus, when
Effie first realises her jealousy :—

" And in that interminable dark advance of
morning she was thinking at five o'clock: ' I
mustn't break my heart with loving you.' She
kept imagining her hand moving across his

hair. ' But that breaks my heart,' she thought, and her first effort at detachment was to forbid herself that imaginary movement of her hand. So she became at war with herself. ' Then I must hold his hand,' she stipulated. ' Well, just his hand, but only for a minute. . . . No, not so tenderly, not such feeling. *Don't you see that breaks your heart, too?* ' "

Though Milly, having lost Clive, accepts a pleasant young man, with whom she manages to find some pleasure, neither sister has any serious thought, or aim, in life outside the " grande passion " : both are curiously hard and selfish towards others, particularly their rather tiresome parents. One forgives them : because their capacities for joy and misery are so intense and vivid, so youthful, and so sincere.

Though in every novel Miss Meynell depends on the one topic and adopts the one manner, there are, of course, variations in the construction. " Second Marriage," for example, is not quite so absolutely dominated by the intimate expression of a girl's love. We have here some record of a man doing man's work, the stubborn reclaiming of fen-land from the encroaching floods; triumphantly persisted in against the prejudice of neighbours, who were satisfied with conditions that were good enough for their fathers. There is a more detailed presentation of family life, here epitomised in three sisters, dissimilar in charac-

ter and experience. We see something of their
neighbours and of a boy's weak spine cured by
a friend's patient devotion. Yet here again,
the tale gradually becomes concentrated upon
a woman's love. One who has married, bril-
liantly but unhappily; and, coming back to her
family, loses her heart to the man they dislike
and distrust. She is more hesitating than most
of Miss Meynell's heroines; love does not, at
first at least, occupy her whole mind : but in the
end she succumbs no less completely. And,
like them, she proves quite incapable of con-
cealing her infatuation. She, too, is entirely
without normal self-restraint.

A whole group of gay young people setting
off on a skating-party know the secret of her
happiness :—

"She looked younger than usual. Her
cheeks were bright with colour, her beautiful
lips parted in her eager expectation, and it was
small wonder if the glances which the
assembled people cast at her awoke vivid
images in every mind, composed partly of what
rumour had told them, and partly suggested
inevitably by the sight of her as she stood
there. They wanted with almost painful
interest that the man she was expecting should
arrive—for to see him come to her and cast one
look at her face would assuredly be the equiva-
lent of witnessing something far more secret
and intimate between two others. Yes; one
look at that face as it now appeared in its

beauty from the man who loved her must be as passionately expressive as the most intimate kisses given to another."

In this instance hope was doomed to disappointment; and, finally, " her long, dogged expectation seemed to break up, leaving her face with a strained, blank, dead look." In all things, at all times, she had become totally indifferent to appearances, utterly careless of what folk might think.

Miss Meynell's heroines, and indeed most of her heroes, seem curiously aloof from real life. To them, apparently, the world scarcely matters. They are strangely and, for the most part rather miserably, wrapped up in one idea, one desire. It hardly enters their minds to think about other people, save only the beloved; to compare their own experiences with others; to consider what people commonly think, or how they act. It is always absolutely their own affair : wherein no other can take part, which no other can ever have experienced. They are themselves the beginning and the end. They approach the mystery by an analysis of their own emotions, by watching their own hearts. They have no pre-conceived notions of human nature to guide them, no inherited instincts, no memory or knowledge of a parallel instance. It is the attitude of childhood : innocent, curious, surprised; often tortured; but never doubting their own position as centre of the universe. Life is simply

" what I do, what I feel, what happens to me."
They are not, at least consciously, egotistical,
because they are not aware that it is possible to
live in, or for, others; they do not deliberately
shut out other considerations, because they
ignore their existence.

It is somewhat perplexing to analyse or to
pronounce upon this atmosphere of unreality.
It is not, certainly, altogether alien to human
nature and, by her sheer sincerity and eagerness, Miss Meynell has put life into her
characters. We are in some way bewitched
into believing in them, taking an interest in
their fate, studying them with affection. They
do not, actually, seem to be either so morbid,
so unnatural, or so foolish as any summary
description must make them appear. Partly, I
think, Miss Meynell's own profound, if naïve,
curiosity about them carries conviction : partly
we welcome their supreme youth. Standing a
little outside life, they perhaps see things
which escape others more actively involved by
ordinary affairs.

There can be no doubt, moreover, that Miss
Meynell believes in her own creations. She
takes them seriously, realises them acutely, and
presents them with a very effective combination
of outspokenness and restraint. She is at
once curiously modern in her acceptance of
emotional facts, curiously old-world in her
simple-minded delicate way of handling them.
She assumes, because she knows, that women

think about love on their own initiative. Being more interested in women, she writes almost exclusively from their point of view. But the attitude is never aggressive, rebellious, or ostentatiously unconventional. She simply takes up opinion where she finds it, and works, to her own ends, on the material at hand. Her gentle precision and modesty are all her own, her courage and independence, her generation's. The combination proves attractive, and is certainly unique.

LOT BARROW -	1913
MODERN LOVERS -	1914
COLUMBINE -	1915
NARCISSUS -	1916
SECOND MARRIAGE	1918

DOROTHY RICHARDSON

DOROTHY RICHARDSON

In many ways Miss Richardson is the most original of all our novelists. Her methods and structure are both new, and absolutely unique.

She has declared herself that: " You ought not to think in words—I mean—you can think in your brain by imagining yourself going on and on through it, endless space. Yet, whether you agree or not, language is the only way of expressing anything, and it dims every-thing."

That is her problem—to coax words into the expression of thought.

Miss Richardson has devoted all her novels to the revelation of one heroine: in itself an achievement to invite criticism and excite re-spect. Nor does there seem any reason why her whole life should not be given to the same effort, since the story can never end. Re-membering, perhaps, the dictum that anyone could write one good novel, the history of his or her own life; she has extended the truth to

its logical conclusion, that anyone could write
many good novels, on the same subject.

Here, in fact is a new form of realism, the
reproduction of life in all the actual minutiae
of our impressions, truthfully reaching the
infinite : while almost wholly ignoring material
events or appearances, all the surface of things.
If you imagine your thoughts and emotions,
thrown on a film, and illustrated by a phono-
graph; it becomes obvious that the " moving
picture " would go on for years—even to three
score and ten.   Inevitably Miss Richardson is
not absolutely literal in this matter.   She does,
in fact, select: does not give us everything;
but she approaches completeness more nearly
than any other writer, and completeness is her
aim.

There is no beginning, middle, or end: no
breaking up into obvious stages—childhood,
youth, etc.: so that, though one suspects her
of grouping incident and thought according to
moods, and though one story actually follows
the other; there is no expectation of finality.
We have none in real life.

We recognise, further, that consistency with
this purpose demands narration in the first
person; though here, again, Miss Richardson
does not actually use Miriam's own words
throughout.   We find sentences, paragraphs,
or pages in monologue (or dialogue), followed
by a narrative passage.   Yet both are, in fact,
Miriam's own thoughts or her own observa-

tions. It is not, indeed, obvious why the variation has been adopted; but it breaks monotony, and emphasises the impression of truth. The passages within inverted commas are in some subtle fashion more intimate and personal. They justify the convention.

All this, inevitably, produces a kind of absolute realism, which is unique. As Mr. Beresford expresses it, (introducing " Pointed Roofs ") she is " the first novelist who has taken the final plunge: who has neither floated nor waded, but gone head under, and become a very part of the human element she has described "—only she never *describes*. Miss Sinclair, also, expresses the same idea: " She must be Miriam Henderson. She must not know or divine anything that Miriam does not divine, she must not see anything that Miriam does not see. She has taken Miriam's nature upon her."

This is a new development of the first-person form. It is the spiritual, and emotional expression of the true realism; the actual ego. " Nothing happens. It is just life going on and on. It is Miriam Henderson's stream of consciousness going on and on."

It is not, perhaps, of great importance to determine whether Miss Richardson's originality is deliberate, whether she has consciously invented a new method and a new manner. She has, in fact, given us something which carries its own reason, its own duties, its own ideal. And she has brought that method (or art) to a singularly high pitch of perfection. It will not probably prove *the* new method of writing a novel: but it is *a* new method (imagined consistently and carried out with success) which will find followers and found a school. We can already detect its influence on several novelists.

There are, of course, certain obvious limitations imposed by the completeness of her reform, which would itself, however, be valueless if it were not complete: and there are details of style and manner which—perhaps needlessly—affront tradition.

In the first place, we hesitate before the triviality of many details. Life, itself, certainly, contains much which is not worth recording. The novelist must select, and Miss Richardson boldly abandons the usual *principle* of selection, which we call composition. She offers us no plot, no finished story: no one philosophy or concentrated moral. She leaves in a great deal generally omitted, and does not reveal any system to guide her choice.

Yet I am confident, for a thousand reasons, that she is, in fact, perfectly aware of what she *must* do, in order to produce what she wishes to achieve. As Miss Sinclair, again, expresses it: "She must not interfere: she must not analyse, or comment, or explain." That is to say; having projected herself into Miriam, she must follow the instincts of Miriam, setting down all that interests Miriam, everything Miriam had noticed or remembered, what she is thinking about. And this is how life seems to us, what we get out of life.

Thus, and thus only, does she reveal character: by Miriam's selection from life. If we are interested in the real Miriam, we should endeavour to understand everything that passes in her mind, all that produces her emotions.

Otherwise, and this, again, is a limitation, though essential to complete realism; Miss Richardson is not concerned with character. She looks no further than Miriam into others, does not reflect their points of view. They are more or less vivid, more or less finished, just as Miriam can, or will, look into them. They appear to us, as they appear to her. This involves not only the limitations from conditions life imposes upon us all—whereby we cannot get really within others—but a further limitation imposed by Miriam's opportunities and her will. Of any character introduced she may say: "I want no more from him. I will not see him, or even think about him, again." If the reader *wants* more, Miss Richardson will not provide it, and for her purpose, she is justified.

Finally, we recognise that certain peculiarities of style are the logical outcome of this ideal. It is not only that Miss Richardson ignores any conventional grammatical construction, except when it comes naturally.

She uses a form of expression which is literally photographic; and goes further than we have seen elsewhere, because it reflects not only conversation (which is often indifferent to grammar) but thoughts—which are still more disjointed. Indeed, in most narrative one feels the supposed utterance of thought is nearly always artificial and clumsy, just because the author translates it into a sentence. Miss Richardson abolishes the sentence: as, in fact, we all do in real life. In this matter she is very courageously literal: covering her pages with dots, dashes, and broken sentences. Also, she boldly sets a full stop after a single word: noun, verb, or adjective. Thus: "'Mps,' said Eve," or again: "His skin was white and clean . . . mat, like felt . . ." This is real thinking aloud; and also she spells her words as we pronounce them: "Ow-de-do?" "adaw" (for adore), "drorinroom," etc.

All of which makes these novels extraordinarily difficult: that is, until they become familiar. One feels unable to catch hold anywhere: to arrange one's conclusions: to praise or condemn. For example, in a sense we know Miriam intimately. We have been through many experiences, met many friends, in her company: we have—in the most real sense—seen life through her mind. Yet one would hesitate either to describe or analyse. Certainly, she does not conform to type.

A few characteristics, however, stand out:
most prominently her abounding delight in
life. This does not appear in the tone of the
narrative which is quiet, fastidious, and critical.
It does not arise from any romance in her
experience. It permits—in one passage—a
decision to commit suicide. It is sprung on
one, suddenly, for no apparent reason, certainly without any sequence of ideas. A sudden flash from the very sanctuary of her
emotions that will out—just because it really
explains everything.

Thus on one occasion she expresses her joy
through sympathy:

" This is how Mag. is feeling. Their kettle
is bumping on their spirit lamp too. She loves
the sound just in this way, the Sunday morning sound of the kettle with the air full of
coming bells and the doors opening—I'm half-
dressed, without any effort—and shutting up
and down the streets is *perfect*, again, and
again: at seven o'clock in the silence, with the
air coming in from the squares, smelling like
the country, is bliss. ' You know, little child,
you've an extraordinary capacity for happiness.' I suppose I have. Well: I can't help it
. . . I *am* frantically, frantically happy. I
Mag has to talk to Jan about the happy things.
Then they go, a little. The only thing to do
is either to be silent or make cheerful noises.
Bellow. If you do that too much, people don't
like it. You can only keep on making cheerful

noises if you're quite alone.   Perhaps that's
why people in life are always grumbling at
' annoyances ' and things; to hide how happy
they are   .   .   .   ' there's a dead level of
happiness all over the world'—hidden. People
go on about things because they are always
trying to remember how happy they are. The
worse things are the more despairing they get,
because they're so happy '   .   .   .   ' They
do things that have nothing to do with their
circumstances.   They were always doing
things like this all the year round.   Spring
and Summer and Autumn and Winter things.
They had done, for years.   The kind of things
that make independent elderly women, widows
and spinsters who were free to go about, have
that look of intense appreciation.' "

Happiness is an "appreciation" of life,
independent of circumstances.   And again:

"Live, don't worry   .   .   .   I've always
been worrying and bothering.   I'm going to
be like Mrs. Kronen: but quite different, because she hasn't the least idea how beautiful
things really are.   She doesn't know that
everyone is living a beautiful strange life, that
has never been lived before.   .   .   .   Her
breakfast was a feast.   .   .   .   Her room was
a great square of happy light   .   .   .   happy,
happy.   .   .   .   Roses in her blood and gold
in her hair   .   .   .   it was something be-
longing to them, something that made them
gleam.   It was her right; even if they gleamed

only for her. They gleamed: she knew it. Youth, the glory of youth. So strong. She had got herself into this beautiful life, found her way into it . . . a secret happy life."

There is, also, a charming naïveté about Miriam's ecstacy when she makes some change in her circumstances. Every new experience is welcomed with vigorous optimism. And, with careful attention; we can learn something of what she actually did; what really happened. The whole, in fact, is a story of freedom and independence, sought and obtained. She left home, because there was not much money, and she must *do* something. She lived, for a time, in a German school; she met some strange people in a family to whom she was a governess; she went to live in a London boarding-house; she took a room of her own, and worked for some, unexpectedly interesting, dentists in Wimpole Street. We know her exact salary, and remember that wonderful day when she got a rise.

Miriam, of course, is impulsive and tender-hearted; yet rather diffident and very sensitive to other people's opinion. I have no doubt that she charmed people (both men and women) but she does not seem to have grasped anyone—definitely or permanently: mainly because at the least friction she would suddenly go away and shut herself up. After all, her life was a " happy secret." She contrives in a mysterious way, to be both extraordinarily

sympathetic—at a crisis, even self-sacrificing—
and yet supremely self-centred. Emphatically
she is not an egoist: only frankly and absorb-
ingly curious and interested about herself.

Like most women (at least, as drawn in
contemporary fiction) she is more easily and
deeply moved by music than by any other
outside influence. Germany taught her what
it means to be really, genuinely musical: and
one of her unexpected flashes of ordinary
humour appears in the clever description of
the *two* ways of playing badly, one innocent,
the other affected. " No English person
would quite understand—the need, that the
Germans understood so well—to admit the
beauty of things . . . the need of the
strange expression of music, making the
beautiful things more beautiful."

Finally, Miss Richardson expresses—more
fully than most women—that curious conviction (which seems to be the latest development
of the sex-problem, as they view it) that men
are, in some sense, outside real life, more on
the surface, more artificial. Because material
events absorb them and they must always be
doing something, they succeed in blinding
themselves to Reality by talking cleverly
about it. Books—and men—kill your soul.

Thus in " Interim " we read of her resolve
for the new year:

" Life would be an endless inward singing
until the end came . . . no more books.

Books all led to the same thing. All the things in books were unfulfilled duties. *No more interest in men.* They shut off the inside world. Women who had anything to do with men were not themselves. They were in a noisy confusion, playing a part all the time. . . . The only real misery of being alone was the fear of being left out of things. It was a wrong fear. It pushed you into things, and then everything disappeared."

Again: "There was no thought in the silence, no past or future, *nothing but the strange thing for which there were no words, something that was always there as if by appointment, waiting for one to get through to it away from everything, away from everything in life.* . . . It was happiness and realisation. It was being suspended, in nothing. It came out of oneself, because it came only when one had been a long time alone. It was not oneself. It could not be God . . . perhaps it was evil. One's own evil genius. But how could it be when it made you so blissful? What was one—what had one done to bring the feeling of goodness and beauty and truth into the patch on the wall, and presently make all the look of the distant world and everything in experience sound like music in a dream?"

Once more: "Happiness crops up before we can prevent it . . . it is my secret companion. Waiting at the end of every dark passage. I did not make it myself. I *can't* help it."

This, then, is Miss Richardson's final philosophy of life, her secret: and whenever she lifts the veil—always disclosing the same Ideal—we find man ruthlessly banished, a permanent exile. It would seem that women have now discovered for themselves a new Reality—a vision and an interpretation: where at present, there is no room for man.

You notice that books are also a hindrance; and, remembering her own striking originality, we are eager to hear more of Miss Richardson's views on literature.

She has said in her wroth, that "novelists are angry men lost in a fog": and she speaks elsewhere of "rows and rows of fine books; nothing but men sitting in studies doing something cleverly, being very important, men of letters, and looking out for approbation. If writing meant that, it was not worth doing . . . if books were written like that, sitting down and doing it cleverly, and knowing just what you were doing, and just how someone else had done it, there was something wrong, some *mannish* cleverness that was only half right. To write books knowing all about style would be to become like a man. Women who wrote books and learned these things would be absurd, and would make men absurd. There was something wrong. It was in all these books upstairs. Good stuff was wrong, a clever trick, not worth doing."

Men make "a story that was like a play, that looked like life when you looked at it, a maddening fussiness about nothing and people getting into states of mind."

Once, however, she describes an author, who certainly suggests her own ideal:

" Each line was wonderful: but all in darkness. Presently on some turned page something would shine out and make a meaning. It went on and on. It seemed to be going towards something. But there was nothing that *anyone* could imagine, nothing in life or the world that could make it clear from the beginning, or bring it to an end. If the man died, the author might stop. *Finis.* But it would not make any difference to anything. . . . It was all one book in some way, not through the thoughts, or the story, but something in the author."

All of which might be applied to Miss Richardson herself.

.   .   .   .

Superficially, it would be almost impossible to imagine a novelist less realistic than Miss Richardson. One could scarcely conceive of a story less dependent upon material observation, upon facts or appearances; less coloured by that ugliness or morbidity which has been so often acclaimed as truth.

Yet, in fact, she is the complete realist. She

has carried the ideal of realism to its last, logical, conclusion: the observation, and reproduction, of thought and emotion. Stepping boldly behind the "poor man with his documents," as Stevenson calls him, she exposes her own soul, unveils what lurks behind life, makes it real. Always looking for what really matters, what we are here for; she reveals reality—not dramatically in theories and dogmas, or abstractions—not as a composed philosophical picture; but just as it actually comes to us, hour by hour, fitfully in odd moments, interrupting, encroaching upon, and —for the time at least—either eclipsing or revealing—the surface of our existence.

She has photographed the soul.

POINTED ROOFS AND PILGRIMAGE	1915
JOY OF YOUTH	1916
BACKWATER	1916
HONEYCOMB	1917
THE TUNNEL	1919
INTERIM	1919

VIRGINIA WOOLF

VIRGINIA WOOLF

MRS. WOOLF, who "sometimes wonders" whether "there's anything else in the whole world worth doing" except writing novels, is quite explicit about the aim of fiction: "what we want to do in writing novels is to find out what's behind things."

Her hero-novelist (in "The Voyage Out") expounds the theory: "Things I feel come to me like lights. . . . I want to combine them. . . . Have you ever seen fireworks that make figures? . . . I want to make figures"; and again, "One doesn't want to do things; one wants merely to be allowed to see things. . . . I want to write a novel about Silence, the things people don't say."

All of which confirms very closely what I have endeavoured to expound concerning Mrs. Woolf's contemporaries. Elsewhere, again, in the same story, she emphasizes the importance of the "facts of life . . . what really goes on, what people feel, although they generally try to hide it. There's nothing to be frightened at. It's so much more beautiful than the pretences—always more interesting—always better, I should say." Yet the problem of expression remains. "You ought to write Music. . . . Music goes straight for things. It says all there is to say at once. In writing it seems to me there's so much scratching on the match-box." Again: "Why don't people write about the things they do feel? Ah, that's the difficulty!"

In her search for facts, for realities, Mrs. Woolf does not actually adopt Miss Richardson's method of self-revelation, but writes from outside as an observer. She is most intimate in dialogue; choosing the instrument, or vehicle, of two lovers honestly endeavouring (without any denial or forgetfulness of the individual sensitiveness between them which made "the sound of their voices so beautiful that by degrees they scarcely listened to the words they framed") to discover each other and to express themselves. Writing primarily as a woman of women, starting—as it were—from the woman's outlook and the girl's curiosity, she does also achieve, with greater subtlety and success than most women novelists, to see into men, or at least a man.

St. John Hirst, indeed, was born a bachelor: "He'd lived all his life in front of a looking-glass, so to speak, in a beautiful panelled room, hung with Japanese prints and lovely old chairs and tables, just one splash of colour,

you know, in the right place,—between the
windows I think it is,—and there he sits hour
after hour with his toes on the fender, talking
about philosophy and God and his liver and
his heart, and the hearts of his friends.
They're all broken. You can't expect him
to be at his best in a ballroom. He wants a
cosy, smoky, masculine place, where he can
stretch his legs out, and only speak when he's
got something to say."

Mrs. Ambrose, on the other hand, concludes
that if women were " properly educated I don't
see why they shouldn't be much the same as
men—as satisfactory, I mean; though, of
course very different."

But with Rachel Willoughby and Terence
Hewet, these questions of men and women are
far more intricate, because of infinite import
ance to themselves. Although content, and
indeed exquisitely happy in their love, they
are most desperately anxious to understand
each other—and human nature.

He maintained " there was an order, a pat-
tern that made life reasonable or, if that word
was foolish, made it of deep interest anyhow;
for sometimes it seemed possible to understand why things happened as they did":
" and she would come to love ten people out
of every twelve when she found they were like
herself."

Womanlike, she realises—earlier than he—
what she wants from him in their individual

relationships: "Why did he sit so near and keep his eye on her? Why did they not have done with this searching and agony? Why did not they kiss each other simply? She wished to kiss him. But all the time she went on spinning out words." Yet, when they had spoken—"We love each other"—she was no less eager to analyse than he.

"It's no good," she had once declared bitterly, men and women "should live separate; we cannot understand each other, we only bring out what's worst." And he admits the conclusion that: "They were different. Perhaps, in the far future, when generations of men had struggled and failed as he must now struggle and fail, woman would be, indeed, what she now made a pretence of being —the friend and companion—not the enemy and parasite of man."

Of the Victorian women she had seen, "their minute acts of charity and unselfishness which flowered punctually from a definite view of what they ought to do, their friendships, their tastes and habits; she saw all these things like grains of sand falling, falling through innumerable days, making an atmosphere and building up a solid mass, a background." Theirs is a profession which Mrs. Woolf also describes in "Night and Day": "Katherine, then, was a member of a very great profession which has, as yet, no title and very little recognition, although the labour of the mill and factory is, perhaps, no more severe and the results of less benefit to the world. *She lived at home.* She did it very well, too.''

Curiously enough, for a woman in love, Rachel claims the privilege which convention accedes to man: '' It seemed to her that she wanted many *more* things than the love of one human being—the sea, the sky.''

Yet, says Terence, were it not for the men who put work and ideal before love of women; '' Rachel herself would be a slave with a fan to sing songs to men when they felt drowsy. ' But you'll never see it,' he exclaimed, ' because with all your virtues you don't, and you never will, care with every fibre of your being for the pursuit of truth! You've no respect for facts. Rachel, you're essentially feminine' ''

Like so many modern young people they are both disposed to be shy of marriage, despite her impatient: '' Oh, our faults, what do they matter? Am I in love—is this being in love—are we to marry each other? ''

In the beginning he could only think of marriage, and home life, as a degradation of the ideal.

'' Partly because he was irritated by Rachel, the idea of marriage irritated him. It immediately suggested the picture of two people sitting alone over the fire ; the man was reading, the woman sewing. There was a second picture.

He saw a man jump up, say good-night, leave
the company and hasten away with the quiet
secret look of one who is stealing to certain
happiness. Both these pictures were very unpleasant, and even more so was the third picture,
of husband and wife and friend ; and the married people glancing at each other as though
they were content to let something pass un-
questioned, being themselves possessed of the
deeper truth. . . . Here were the worn husband and wife sitting with their children round
them, very patient, tolerant, and wise. . . .
He saw them always, walled up in a warm,
firelit room . . . on the other hand, unmarried people he saw active in an unlimited
world . . . all the most individual and
humane of his friends were bachelors and spinsters ; indeed, he was surprised to find that the
women he most admired, and knew best, were
unmarried women. Marriage seemed to be worse
to them than it was for men.''

When the lovers can talk it over together,
however, marriage seems more adventurous:

" I shall be in love with you all my life, and
our marriage will be the most exciting thing
that's ever been done! We'll never have a
moment's peace——" " Well, then, what will
it be like when we're married ? " she asks.
" What I like about your face," he began, " is
that it makes one wonder what the devil you're
thinking about—it makes me want to do that,"
he clenched his fist and shook it so near her that

she started back, " because now you look as if
you'd blow my brains out. There are moments,"
he continued, " when, if we stood on a rock
together, you'd throw me into the sea."

Hypnotised by the force of his eyes in hers,
she repeated, " If we stood on a rock together——"

To be flung into the sea, to be washed hither
and thither, and driven about the roots of the
world—the idea was incoherently delightful.
She sprang up and began moving about the
room, bending and thrusting aside the chairs
and tables as if she were indeed striking through
the waters. He watched her with pleasure; she
seemed to be cleaving a passage for herself, and
dealing triumphantly with the obstacles which
would hinder their passage through life.

It would be difficult, I think, to find two
passages in which the true philosophy of marriage has been more suggestively set forth.
The first, conventional, conception sees no
more than surface values—that which appears
to happen: which, if we refuse to recognise a
meaning in life beyond the material, will be
acclaimed the real truth and, which—because
we so believe—may for us at least, become
final. It is impossible to obtain more from
life, or from each other, than we seek. The
second picture, for all its odd whimsicality,
does reveal, very dramatically, the great adventure: that wonderful mystery of all Romance which illumines the world with every-

thing unexpected, all that hidden glory it may be given us to invade and conquer, those joys which courage and happiness may bring to the Soul of man—when true love opens the door. Only to some, and to them only sometimes, is it given to step within; but they find Truth.

"It seemed to Rachel that her sensations had no name"; but Mrs. Woolf has given us —over her whole narrative—a true revelation of "falling in love" and of loving; which almost denies her own statements about the difficulty of expressing what we feel. These young people are, indeed, most amazingly frank: but neither unpleasant, cynical, nor morbid. Because, for all their talking and curiosity, they are at bottom perfectly natural, healthy-minded, and frankly happy. They say everything which one is accustomed, rather scornfully, to call "modern"; and yet they are essentially normal and even sensible. One has no feeling that they are wasting life, or arguing away their own chances of having a good time. Mrs. Woolf has mingled Romance with the new Realism and, in so doing, solves many of the problems which are vexing us to-day. She does not fear the truth, but she has the vision.

Wherefore I find it difficult to forgive her having permitted Rachel to die, just when she had grasped happiness, of a fever caught through an idle pleasure trip. It is, of course, one way of finishing the story. Clearly, there

remains no more to be said.   But there would
have been no less art, and equal truth, in
leaving these two vital young people to the
perfect understanding they do, in fact, actually
achieve: and trusting the reader's imagination
concerning a future of which they had every
reason to hope.   I do not understand the weakness which has led Mrs. Woolf to succumb to
the prevailing taste for tragedy as the end of
fiction.   Here, at least, it is out of focus; and
seems introduced with a kind of jerk.   It
throws back the reader from the absorbing
topic of its central motive, into the surface
interests of the tale; which are, indeed, many
and quite attractive, but of secondary value.

It may seem perverse to Mrs. Woolf, but
I confess that I could, more willingly, have
accepted tragedy in " Night and Day," where
all the elements for such a conclusion are—
most obviously—present.

Here the coming together of Ralph and
Katherine is beset with difficulties—far more
dangerous than mere circumstances—which
seem well-nigh insuperable.   Their mutual
revelations of thought and character have no
courageous spontaneity, as had Rachel's.
They are, for the most part, forced, veiled
by sub-conscious hostility, never *quite* sincere
or whole-hearted; approached with hesitation,
and coloured by doubt.   Here, too, we meet
with the social triangle; for, without question,
Katherine and Denham were vastly intrigued

by each other—apart from the troublesome relations between Ralph and Mary.

The poise of fate, in fact, is most delicately balanced, and, by a thousand accidental misunderstandings or acts of folly, might have been overset. The conclusion is welcomed, but not inevitable. Here true happiness, nearly missed, was possible; and happiness came.

It should be added, however, that what conventionality calls the love-interest, which means, at its best, an intimate revelation of youth, does not so fully dominate this novel. It gives us a most interesting addition to the pictures, noticed in earlier chapters, which contemporary fiction contains, of professional literary life, and serious journalism.

Katherine was born in a legendary atmosphere of High Art. Her home was a shrine: subtly dedicated to memory: "Above her nursery fireplace hung a photograph of her grandfather's tomb in Poet's Corner." Much of her time was spent helping her mother to produce a life of the great poet. . . . The book must be written. It was a duty that they owed to the world.

As meanwhile, her father—Mr. Hilbery— was the editor of a distinguished Review, and the family atmosphere was impregnated with literature: literary men and women were the familiars of the house. William Rodney, again, was a poet and critic—fastidious, but not flabby;

whose artistic enthusiasms were absolutely sincere. Ralph was a writer of sound ability: and if Mary was more at home with causes than causeries, she, too, had the literary sense. Mrs. Woolf does not write on this matter with the intensity of Miss Sinclair in "The Creators," or of Miss Dane in "Legend"; but she knows her world no less intimately, and her touch is no less assured. She has given us "the real thing," and its peculiar charm must hold all who love books or aspire to write them. There is a sense, of course, in which the "professional" author stands somewhat aloof from life, having his own sense of values: but, for the larger minds, this enclosure is not narrow or false or affected. The persons of this drama, in fact, are both real and attractive as human beings, the somewhat choice flavour of their utterances does not disguise emotion, and their charm possesses its own genuine appeal. Once more the relations between parents and child, between love and friendship, are sympathetically treated in their only legitimate application: as they affect the individuals concerned, not as a general problem in psychology, to be determined by dogma.

"Night and Day," in a word, belongs to contemporary fiction, illuminating the subjects and questions with which the novelists of to-day are mainly concerned. holding its own with the best,

"Her romance," said Katherine, "was a desire, an echo, a sound; she could drape it in colour, see it in form, hear it in music, but not in words; no, never in words."

Like her contemporaries, it would seem that, if Mrs. Woolf has been "teased" by ideals of art, "so incoherent, so incommunicable," she, too, recognises that to attain them is to achieve.

THE VOYAGE OUT - 1915
NIGHT AND DAY - 1919

STELLA BENSON

II

STELLA BENSON

OUR first impressions of Miss Stella Benson
are rather bewildering : bewildering, because
while she has an exceptionally firm grip of
realities, her heart dwells with the unreal.
" I Pose " was principally concerned with
plain men and women, playing a part indeed,
but subject to the ordinary limitations of
humanity. " This is the End " revealed a
strange commingling of war-time flesh and
blood characters with a marvellous dream-life
of the sea-shore : of " Living Alone " she
writes frankly : " This is not a real book. It
does not deal with real people, nor should it
be read by real people."
The pioneer women-novelists all practised
realism, as their contribution to the historical
development of English fiction : realism, again,
was certainly the prevalent note of late nine-
teenth century writers. Those of the twentieth
have not escaped the tradition : but some of
them have imposed thereon a new mysticism
(perhaps the most interesting aftermath of war-

mentality) which seems to indicate at once looking backward and straining ahead. At present
this does not amount to a new philosophy of
life; though Miss Benson, for example, can reflect and generalise. She declares that " one
dies as one lives, in a little ordinary way, and
that there is no glory between people who
don't lie to one another." She sees " the whole
world as a thing running away from its
thoughts ": and (like Clemence Dane in
" Legend ") she finds " nothing in the world
but second bests."

Finally, in " Living Alone," there is some
hint of a general solution :—

" Everyone," says Richard, the Man of
Magic, " sees something lacking about the Victorian age," and " obviously what was wrong
with the last century was just that it didn't
believe in fairies. . . . This century knows
that it doesn't know everything . . . we
have started a new spell . . . magic has
risen again to meet the war."

Ours to-day, then, is the knowledge of ignor-
ance; and, certainly, one could imagine no
more complete reaction against the complacency of the Victorians and their confident
materialism. It contributes, however, to our
unrest.

It would be obviously unreasonable to expect any complete or ordered philosophy from
youth : while the world is in the melting-pot.
Miss Benson, indeed, is not essentially a

revolter—like her " suffragette "; though she
does not accept convention, authority, or tradition. A complete view of her attitude leaves
rather the impression of one dissatisfied,
though sympathising, with average humanity—
as represented by " the Family " : a wanderer
not without hope : seeking somewhere in the
" Parish of Faery " (with which she is not altogether unfamiliar) for something that may
prove at least more satisfying, if not actually
an interpretation.

It is possibly to emphasise the beautiful possibilities of this beautiful dream-world, that
she has introduced (in all three novels) the
vivid atmosphere of Brown Borough; where
true " palliness " means " a drop and a jaw
together."   And here, strangely enough, she
seems thoroughly at home. Whether it be
through the Suffragettes' honest attempt at up-
lifting (poisoned by clerical interference);
through Jay's genial ambition to " 'urry and
get drunk " with Mrs. Love, and " keep 'and
in 'and all the time "; or through the " Com-
mittee " and Sarah Brown's office for "collect-
ing evidence from charitable spies about the
naughty poor "; Miss Benson knows these
people and those, officially or unofficially, at
work among them. Just as always and everywhere, despite a flavour of aloofness or in-
humanity, she loves children with understanding; she is equally at home with East End
Girls' Clubs, the men and women of the

"mean streets," or the Vicar who honestly
regards Trades Unions (at least for women)
as a wile of the devil. It is, I think, really
an admirable study in understanding to
compare Jay's true comradeship in the joys
of the slum-life, with the sorrows and tragedies
which the Suffragette strives to relieve. To
understand Happiness is more difficult, and
quite as helpful, as to sympathise with grief.
It is a rare gift.

One may notice, in passing, that Miss
Benson has, no doubt unconsciously, followed
the wisdom of the pioneers. Like Jane Austen
and other great early women novelists, she only
attempts to exhibit this rare insight for her own
sex. Here she writes as a woman for women,
and the limitation is most prudent. It ensures
success. We do not, indeed, claim for her any
power that is positively unique. Other writers
understand " the Poor "—individually. But
it is remarkable in Miss Benson, because of her
strong leanings towards mysticism, and the
curious position of her other character-types.
She can observe and reflect.

The persons in " I Pose," indeed, cannot be
fitted into any pigeon-hole. They are, fortunately, as far removed from the typical
" modern " (with its obsession for sex and its
passion for ugliness) as from the Victorian
" sentimental." But, superficially, they live
much like ordinary folk : their experiences are
human, if unusual. They are, indeed, born

tramps—though more addicted to " passing by " than to adventure; having no special interest in Savages, Super-men, or the Antique; no craving for Wild Lands or Lone Seas.

In " This is the End " and " Living Alone," Miss Benson seems to have discovered a new country and, if one may so express her, a new humanity. It is neither the nursery land of genii and princesses, the haunted shadowland of W. B. Yeats, nor the Home of the Gods. We meet here with horses and suit cases, dogs and broomsticks, who can talk : and at least one dragon, strangely employed as foreman to faery farm-labourers. The unconventional witch rides a conventional broomstick : the man of magic produces thunderstorms, and travels " by flash of lightning " : a mayor is rendered invisible.

Speaking generally, the human characters here are happier than most; because they possess the secret of two lives—one material, the other visionary. And it is in their dreams they are most themselves. Jay and her brother speak gaily enough of lying to other people : but one can be sure they do not themselves regard the " House by the Sea " as a lie. For them it has more substance and greater value than their obvious, every-day, life : though its symbolism remains obscure. So far, indeed, as Mr. Russell is permitted a glimpse of this secret Paradise, it seems to figure his lost youth, to hint at what " might have been." It enables him, at least, to forget the " woman who had not properly realised the fact that she was Mrs. Russell." And " The House " actually visited by Anonyma is no more than a frank revival of nurseryland, created of poignant war fever to which (as also shown elsewhere) Miss Benson is very much alive.

But even to Jay herself the " Secret " is, after all, somewhat shadowy and wavering—not quite dissimilar to those grand dreams of Peter Ibbotson and " The Brushwood Boy." It is haunted by ghosts—of a Friend, dim chambers, fair flowers, and the ocean breeze. It is in " Living Alone " that we find the dramatis personæ of Elfland, the individual magicians (witch and magic-man); the " very plebeian and forward female fairies " between the bean rows. We feel that now Miss Benson has actually visited the " Parish," acquired familiarity with the landscape, and talked to the inhabitants. Her descriptions are now dramatic and vivid, artfully realised, and pictured like real life : without hesitation, firmly outlined.

The visitors—from an air-raided graveyard; the fight in mid-air between a German and the English witch (with their queer quarrel about " who caused the war "); the eager hoeing of Sarah Brown; the " Happiness " sold in a general shop; and the house " with no modern comfort whatever "; seem no more than perfectly legitimate, if unusual, items of local

colour. They create an atmosphere, which is
essential to all fiction; colouring the characters,
but not excluding humanity. They are visible to
quite commonplace folk of varying experience,
culture, and outlook—from every class. They
are described, deliberately, in plain prose; with
all the irrelevant detail and inconsequence of
real life. They just happen.

We are offered, indeed, an escape from the
more sordid and soul-destroying incidents of
civilisation, a home of rest, spiritual happiness,
and some measure of content. But we are not
uplifted to moral rapture, pure poetry, or the
glory of romance. Only the " Spell " is there :
actually present with us : a Gift from the Un-
seen made visible.

Here Miss Benson has given us something
which we cannot find, and never have known,
elsewhere : a new landscape in fiction, a new
creation of art : which, if not normal, is yet a
positive contribution to human experience and
the possible developments of human nature; a
new hint towards the Mystery of the Soul—
not like the frankly inhuman legends of faery,
the idle vision of a dream.

To such unconventional material, obviously,
it is not easy to apply the ordinary critical
tests. Like all reformers, Miss Benson adopts
certain mannerisms which really deform her
art. It is, for example, as she herself says of
Jay, a mere " trick " to christen " one's cigar-
ette," an umbrella, or a " little occasional

pleurisy pain—called Julia '' ; while indicating the actual persons of the tale by class-terms like " the gardener " and the " suffragette." Most of her characters, indeed, *have* christian (and sur) -names : but this, too often, only increases the confusion between the human, the animal, and the inanimate; which—after all— has some significance even in magic.

The majority of modern writers do not aim at style in the conventional sense; and, as indicated already, Miss Benson may have a specific reason, quite justifiable, for adopting the colloquial jerkiness which her contemporaries seem to have learnt from America. Nevertheless, she would be none the worse for more careful grammar, and for some of that composed dignity which we of the older days have been used to consider essential to good writing. This she could clearly accomplish with ease, as one sees from the poetry interspersed and from several poetic passages of description. The truly imaginative have always—style.

Miss Benson, however, does not neglect construction. " I Pose " is put together and completed with a vigorous feeling for drama. It is a finished tale, the record of characters developed consistently to an inevitable denouement. Even in " This is the End " we have a *contained* episode, and " Living Alone " leaves off at the end. Nevertheless, the conventionality, here, may be more apparent than real. Certainly, the gardener and the suffra-

gette pass through the stages proper to fiction,
or drama :—antipathy, attraction, misunderstanding, and tragedy—on the eve of an happy
ending. Like the ordinary hero and heroine,
they suffer mainly from the (well-meaning or
malicious) interference of outsiders. In " This
is the End," again, Jay has her dreams (amid
sordid surroundings, following the Family
split) and, after the shock of her brother's
death, marries the rather " impossible " lover
—a thoroughly good sort—whom in her
moments of exaltation, she had found inade-
quate. " Living Alone," too, is a complete
episode—of magic, vividly war-inspired : for,
on the last page, Sarah Brown " collected
David her dog and Humphrey her suit-case
. . . and stepped over the threshold into
the greater House of Living Alone."

In this matter, then, Miss Benson is less independent than many of her contemporaries.
Having handled a topic, she finishes with it:
having exhibited a character, or an episode, she
closes it. She does not merely stop. Only her
sense of proportion is rather uncertain. The
central figure wanders, rather frequently, into
a bye-path. Important issues are introduced,
and remain ragged.

Miss Benson, however, is well-equipped in
what may be called the paraphernalia of fiction.
She has very considerable humour—on original
methods; and much aptness in turning a
phrase. Even her generalities, which as a

rule the novelist does well to avoid, often suggest real thought. She is sympathetically observant—for all her waywardness—and her dialogue is dramatic. If you accept the characters (and criticism should rather accept than demand) you will admit that their talk is revealing and, nearly always, inevitable. Constantly we come upon the epigram that arrests : " Death is just an ordinary old thing, no more romantic than anything else, without a capital letter " : " to be clever is to share a secret and a smile with all clever people " : " He was so simple that he did his best without thinking about it." Everywhere the point of view is quite clear and quite individual.

And finally I would maintain the apparent paradox that Miss Benson derives her strength from her humanity. However unusual her characters, however unique their experience, they are real people. Whether or no she would repudiate the applause, she does fulfil the true functions of all art—which are to tell a tale and to give pleasure. And part of that pleasure is (consciously or unconsciously) produced by good art; pervading and overmastering the superficial perversities of artifice.

There are, after all, certain standards in all creation : there are legitimate comparisons to be made, not altogether philistine : there are " the unities." Fiction, admittedly, is more flexible than other literature. We moderns indeed have been rather *hurried out of the traces*, in this matter, by our American cousins. To-day we are over-enamoured of the jerk and the gasp : we adore strong language, we abhor the rule. Style has hidden herself under the curtain of realism: and meanwhile the atmosphere and the sources of fiction have expanded in all directions. The novel has become quite shapeless and all-embracing.

Yet something remains; a figment of art which is indestructible, if it eludes definition. And by that standard, always instinctively recognised, Miss Benson can keep her footing. She does—in essence—conform.

Her emotions are poignant, because they are neither over-analysed nor naked. She is, of course, introspective, or she would not be modern : but, on the other hand, she is not morbid or uncouth. At times, she would seem out of touch with the actual and, in moments of egoism, loses her sense of proportion : but she responds at once to simplicity and the kind act. The Gardener and the Suffragette, for example, are always tender and playful with children: they are, indeed, tender and playful with each other—when true to their best selves. Their thwarted ambitions, their love and their despair, even her suicide; are brought about by the actual perversity of real life. They belong to the Heart of Manhood : not drug- or sex-dominated, but vital and human. Jay and her brother, again, are rather exceptionally kind to average humanity, and their dreams are pure romance. Even Richard and the witch have human moments. The minor, or incidental characters are quite frankly normal, and normally observed : and their contrast with hero or heroine rests on differences, not in nature, but in circumstance and vision.

It would not, in fact, be at all just to speak of Miss Benson as an unhealthy writer. Being fortunately quite feminine, she—still more fortunately—does not worry herself about the Decadent or the Super-man. There is a spring, a flush, and a gusto about her work which is positively refreshing. Without ignoring, or failing in sympathy with, the world's heart ache; she has given us a new youth, hopeful for all its puzzlement over cheap ugliness, wasted chances, and cruel stupidity. Missing the full-blooded Chestertonian optimism, she is yet mistress of secret occasions for happiness, somewhat akin to J. M. Barrie's. Though, may be, a little vague about right and wrong, rather uncertain about the whence and the whither; because she dreams of real men and of real women, her dreams are strong.

I POSE   -   -   1917
THIS IS THE END   1917
LIVING ALONE   -   1919

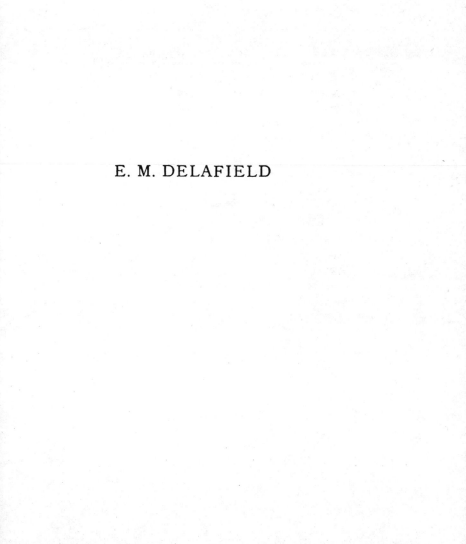

E. M. DELAFIELD

E. M. DELAFIELD

THERE is a certain competent serenity about
Miss Delafield's work which excludes her, perhaps, from the ranks of those who are—rather
aggressively " new " in their manner. Though
actually a " war-product " and, in one novel at
least, humourously intent upon the lighter
psychology of war, she does not like most of
her contemporaries — write with the new
subtlety of analysis, from the soul outwards.
Like the conventional novelist she relates,
while they speak. Her four stories are
observed, composed, and presented in the
normal manner of fiction : where the author
permits herself to see inside all her characters
—as one cannot in real life. They are not the
actual utterances of one tortured soul, who can
only interpret life through her own experience :
but, on the other hand, she is—like the others
—most frankly feminine : always revealing the
woman's outlook, gently satirical upon the fact
that " gentlemen "—as Aunt Marianne so

naïvely expresses it—"do not always think quite as we do about these things"; i.e. about anything.

It has been noticed already that in women-novelists, the analysing habit is very frequently devoted to the study of egoism; and Miss Delafield's Zella affords the most striking example of this tendency : not quite so intense as Miss Dane's studies, but equally subtle.

"Zella," indeed, "sees herself" clearly at all times; and the comparative indifference of other people about this fascinating topic constitutes her main grudge against life. For she *is* fascinating (therein lies the triumph of Miss Delafield) and, in reality, quite astonishingly dependent upon public opinion. In fact, the type of egoism is very original, and most exceptionally attractive. Zella is governed—not only in action but even in thought—by a very passion for adaptability. She demands always to be in the " centre of the picture "; but she expects to *find* this position by absolutely conforming to type; doing and thinking just exactly what people wish, and expect, her to do. The effort leads, naturally, to failure and confusion, because no two people expect at all the same thing : and, in her case, the difficulty is to emerge with emphasis through the dramatically opposed standards and tastes of her nearest relations and her most intimate friends. It may seem a strange thing to say of a confirmed egotist : but the real difficulty about Zella is to discover whether she has any individuality at all, really her own.

Treating, as many of our contemporary women seem to prefer, only the beginnings of life; Miss Delafield leaves Zella " still on the threshold " echoing " the question of ages: what is Truth? " and yet the girl-heroine has, after all, a clearly defined, easily recognised character, humourously portrayed. She " gets at " the reader; so that we utterly sympathise with her childlike eagerness to impose herself upon her surroundings, to enter into the realities, to *be* somebody. She possesses one side of the artistic temperament (which is always attractive, if difficult) : being a born actress, an inveterate *poseur*, more or less self-conscious : and just because, superficially, one can " see through her " so easily, we cannot avoid loving the real Zella under the pathos of her most naïve affectations, and sympathising with every one of her most ridiculous, but quite serious, attempts at asserting herself. The key of the position lies here : that whereas most of us are, at least fairly often and at our best moments, content with being what God made us : she is perpetually engaged in the quite hopeless task of trying to *make herself* into something she was never intended to be.

All this is, obviously, an extreme case of the romance-craving common to all young people —an almost inevitable phase in the develop-

ment of character : but if one can accept the
paradox—Zella charms one because she is
always sincere. She has the gift of all true
artists, that she does really enter into the self-
imposed mood, actually feels and is—for the
moment—all she appears to be. Only because
others are less quick and sensitive—more
" set " along a precise line, they generally
deem her affected. Thus, in the end, Miss
Delafield would have us believe, she may not
only see, but find, herself : since she had learnt
that they—who had influenced her—" had one
and all, conviction at the back of them. She,
afraid and alone, had none. Again and again
she had tampered with something real, and to
her it had not been real."

Miss Delafield, like the others, believes in
Reality—somewhere. That is what she tries,
everywhere, to express.

Again, in " Consequences," and " The Pelicans," she penetrates into the back of things.
The fascinating sisters in " The Pelicans "
have each their own mystery : their strain towards what life and " the others " fail to recognise, it would seem : whence they perpetually
divert. To Francie, indeed, comes rest and
finality : from serene submission to perfect
Faith. For her the convent is peace, death,
fulfilment; not easily attained, indeed, but with
a strangely gentle determination, which is at
once cruel and kind. Never beaten by opposition, always certain of *her* Reality; she dares

even to accept Love's Sacrifice : seeing only the Right, she has the courage to hurt.

And Rosamond, her mother-devotion cut through, baffled and for a time at least torn in shreds by the very passion of revolt, learns her lesson at last. Loving that little sister through whom alone life *meant* anything to her, she yet stumbles, hesitating, out of chaos into the Light. "You see, for *Francie* to do or say anything that hurt *me* was the greatest sacrifice that she could ever have offered," and "there is only one thing that counts, and that's loving, and loving is giving."

Thus understanding, she gives herself—to the man who loves her. For Francie, it was an end; for her a Beginning : but it was one and the same gift.

Fate in "Consequences," indeed, is more freakish. Whether child or woman, Alex could never "fit in" anywhere. She has all Zella's impetuosity for throwing herself into a part, without the artist's enjoyment of the performance. Having a dangerous insight towards her own instability; fully alive to the tragedy of loving, without understanding, other people; always aware of her own baffling "wrongness," and the impossibility to conform : she never escapes "the muddle" of things. Experimenting—as Zella had done—in the haven of Romanism, and (unlike Francie) equally without conviction; she struggles from one failure to another; with

that infinite pathos of the unpractical idealist
with no fixed ideal, which produces, inevitably,
the most deadening of all tragedies : a tragedy
without meaning and grandeur : that need
never have happened, and leads nowhere.
" After all, she had nothing much to live for,
poor Alex. She'd got out of touch with all of
us—and she had no one of her very own." It
was a sister's epitaph !

Such in outline are the central motives, or
inspirations, of Miss Delafield's three first
novels : but she does not depend, exclusively,
upon the central framework. However intense
or subtle the main idea; it is always—with her
—embroidered, and enriched, by the craft of
the normal novelist. She has, to begin with, a
rich fund of humour extending beyond the
mere phrase to her conception of character.
She is as masterly in the painting of an atmosphere as of an individual; because she not only
observes, but interprets. She re-creates life in
its entirety, not as a mere setting for her
heroine, but as it actually moves round every
one of us with all its baffling complexities that
may stand alone, as it were, for a time and
then suddenly (through incidents most trivial
or most dramatic) interfere to spur or to de-
press. The conventions—in Zella—as represented by Mrs. Lloyd-Evans—have little in
common with the exasperating " family " who
torture Alex: yet both are *true* ; while the
varied experiences of Zella—from her artist

father and the French grandmère—do colour
the atmosphere which is drab to Alex. In
" The Pelicans," again, the Family itself is as
abnormal as the heroine : blank to her, indeed,
but quite amazingly wide-minded and receptive to youth in general and to many of its
imaginings. The minor persons themselves
have their own problems, their own pose—
mark the very original relations between Nina
Severing, song-writer, and her son Morris ;
linked to Ludovic and his mother, still more
closely associated with the incomparable wisdom of cousin Bertie.

There is everywhere, again, the broad
foundation of a compact plot, that story-struc-
ture which both separates and joins sound
fiction to real life : usually regarded as the
first test of a good novel; what one may call
the mark of the expert.

And in " The War Workers," where alone
the author evokes, what, in fact, overshadowed
the period of her productiveness, she seems to
depend almost entirely upon such side-issues,
the artifice in her form of expression. True
that here, again, Miss Vivian certainly occupies
the centre of the picture : an egoist of the first
water (almost a " study " for Miss Clemence
Dane's full-length portrait of the one and only
Clare Hartill) : but she is, after all, only a
" personage " in her own eyes : and the art of
the tale comes from its *tout ensemble*. It is
not, perhaps, surprising that Miss Delafield,

like all her contemporaries, has not attempted
the psychology of War. We have here only
the fringe: its effect on those who are in it, but
not of it: those who met the crisis by different
" changes " of viewpoint, largely hysterical;
crowding out thought by hustle. Satire pre-
vails, though the picture is not unkindly. Char
Vivian, indeed, is a martyr of sorts : her sufferings are real enough—like her efficiency in
organisation—but they are self-inflicted and
self-centred.

Miss Delafield has attempted no more than
a sketch, or " turn " as they say in stageland—
wherein the surface of unrest provides atmosphere; and women—at any rate—having lost
their bearings, are burying themselves under
" doing their bit." There is, of course, adroit
sympathy and unsparing satire : the observation is sound and brisk—for the author is an
expert : but the work reveals no more than
craft, an easily used instinct for competent
handling of an attractive episode. It could
scarcely, perhaps, have been better done; but
does not seem quite worth doing.

ZELLA SEES HERSELF - 1917
THE PELICANS -   - 1918
THE WAR-WORKERS - 1918
CONSEQUENCES   - 1919

CLEMENCE DANE

CLEMENCE DANE

Miss Clemence Dane is pre-eminently an artist: neither a preacher nor a philosopher. "Legend," indeed, is a really remarkable *tour de force.* To interest the reader through nearly two hundred pages of *one continuous conversation* upon one subject, between a few friends, is an achievement demanding very rare qualities of style and concentration. Through its unbroken continuity, indeed, the book becomes occasionally breathless, though it moves deliberately. It is distinguished throughout.

There is, properly speaking, no story or plot: yet in the end narrator and onlooker understand each other, with even the hint of a conventional "happy ending." In reality this dramatic conclusion is subtly woven within the whole dialogue: though, superficially, irrelevant to it.

Upon this daringly simple constructive background we are invited to hear a few

clever people talking cleverly about a friend who has just died. Madala Grey, novelist, had always been something of a mystery to her intimates. The woman, and her work, affected them variously—according to their own temperaments. After the first obvious impression of startling originality and outspoken realism in her two first novels: she had puzzled everyone by turning simple and early Victorian in "The Resting Place": and by marrying a "mere man." And now, though no more than twenty-six, she has died: and they must make up their minds. No more evidence being available, the fragments must be gathered up, sorted together, composed into a character.

Most of all, is the process of rounded interpretation imperative for Anita Serle; the "barren" woman with "eyes" and "claws," who when she read Madala Grey's first manuscript, cried to herself: "I'll take my chance. I'll take this genius. I'll make her fond of me. I'll help her. I'll worm myself into her. I'll abase myself. I'll toady. I'll do anything. But I will find out how she does it. I will find out the secret. I'll find it, and I'll make it my own."

And, in the passion of her egoism, she did . . . "carry on like grim death," to achieve conquest:

"I can't make life as Madala can. But— I can take a living thing. I can cut it open

alive. That's what I shall do with this life-
maker—this easy genius. I've taken her to
pieces flesh and blood, bone and ligament and
muscle, every secret of her mind and her
heart and her soul. The life, the *real* life of
Madala Grey, the rise and fall of her genius,
that's what I'm going to make plain. She's
been a puzzle to you all, with her gifts and
her ways and her crazy marriage—she's not a
mystery to me. I tell you I've got her naked,
pinned down, and now I shall make her again.
Isn't it fair?   .   .   . She chose to kill herself. What right had she to take risks? I—
I've refrained. She couldn't. She threw
away her lamp. But I—I take it. I light it
again. Finding's keeping. It's mine."

So to the frenzy of her Boswell-passion, the
others minister not quite spontaneously, perhaps: but drawn in and fascinated by the
subject, dominated by a strong will. Each
has her or his, own mite of memory or suggestion to contribute. All have loved, and
admired, Madala after a fashion. They have
known a little, thought a little, cared a little.
Their curiosity responds. Their cleverness is
stimulated. They offer comment. They become rivals in subtlety of interpretation.

And through her incessant utterance, her
flowing stream of anecdote, reminiscence, and
furious enquiry, Anita will miss nothing.
While holding herself so immeasurably their
superior in knowledge and in understanding,

she will not overlook one contribution, however trivial, they yet may stumble upon. She
is as ready to discuss as to dictate.

For, as the mystery unfolds itself, we learn
that even Anita, the chosen confidant, has in
reality been baffled by her best friend. There
are emotions somewhere she cannot fathom;
experiences she suspects, but cannot establish
—on which her curiosity is aflame. She
probes everywhere without remorse: she cannot suffer reticence, is scarcely superior to
scandal.

Then, finally, lurking in shadow behind and
around the hard brilliance of this keen intellectual analysis, this morbid soul-stripping;
we recognise the soothing presence of Two
who understand. For Jenny Summers (cousin
and secretary to Anita) and for Kent Rehan
(artist who loved Madala) most of this chat-
tering, masked as super-subtlety, is sheer
torture. Only once in a way we hear their
voices; but to them we know, it is given to
see the truth: and, in their silence, slowly and
mysteriously, we watch them drawing together
into their inheritance—"of a widening and
golden future."

For Madala, Jenny declares at last, "had
been a sort of star to you all—a symbol—a
legend," only her husband, "the thing she
married"—had recognised and held the real
woman, who was Madala. And to Kent she
had once striven to show him "what a woman

one day would be to him ": someone a little
like her, certainly, but not herself.

" Do you know—it's strange—you remind
me of her. You are very like her," he
answered.

Elsewhere, again, Miss Dane has given
herself to the egoist. Justin, in " First the
Blade," is the complete masculine: a creature
inured to worship, and blind to criticism. He
is simply incapable of imagining himself not
supreme. And yet he has charm. Clare
Hartill (the feminine counterpart in " Regiment of Women ") is more unusual, possibly
a little strained. This may be, only, however,
that she is revealed more intimately. In these
books, the women are more completely " given
away " than the men. Moreover, Clare is
absolutely driven upon herself, as Justin was
not. In the man, egoism is produced by direct
spoiling, being accepted universally as the
centre of his own world. In the woman, it
is born of solitude: a strong soul naturally
dominant, but cruelly poised alone.

The chief worshipper, at either shrine, is in
the end, inevitably somewhat disillusioned:
but curiously enough, for Laura, without
Justin life had no promise, while Alwynne
gained the world when she lost Clare: it is
Clare dethroned who offers the Supreme
Tragedy.

" First the Blade," indeed, is sub-titled " a
comedy of Growth," and Miss Dane reminds

us that she only offers a story of youth. She
hints finally that in the fulness of time Justin
" will come back to " Laura, chastened and
widened immeasurably by his experience of
War: which is to make a man of him. Boys,
after all, acquire the manners of maturity long
before character. On the other hand, " Regiment of Women " carries finality. Clare will
never gain, because she always exacts. Knowing herself a poseur, seeing her soul's ugliness;
she can never resist exposing herself to those
who worship her: demanding for her worst self
all the devotion they have given enthusias-
tically to her best. It would be difficult to
imagine a more repulsive personality, or one
more poignantly pathetic. In killing another's
soul, she commits moral suicide. It is remorseless waste.

We need not, however, accept the " Regiment of Women " as no more than the full-
length portrait of an unusual heroine. It is
a most intimate revelation of life in a girl's
school: it might even be described as a treatise
on Education; though many of the evils so
vigorously exposed here have been, to a
large extent, realised and removed from more
modern establishments. The main current of
Miss Dane's most righteous indignation, is
directed against the dangers of a society which
regards itself as all-sufficient for human character—at least in youth—and is exclusively
feminine. Wherefore Alwynne escapes to

salvation, in the comradeship of a somewhat
ordinary young man typically masculine.

But though all the teachers suffer in some
degree, primarily, Clare herself; the danger is
obviously far greater for the girls. Miss
Dane, it is clear, has had occasion to feel most
intensely about the poisonously insidious per-
version of youth—and the proper happiness of
youth—which may be so easily effected by an
over-dose of enthusiasm. Clare Hartill, by
her alternative spoiling and sneering at,
favourite pupils; creates around her a thoroughly morbid atmosphere of mental and
emotional strain. The girls are driven to
excessive concentration upon their work,
stirred by the generous impulse to please their
wonderful mistress, which warps their whole
nature. Then, when it pleases her to turn and
rend them—with biting sarcasms—for faults or
stupidity which she has no right to condemn;
they are driven even more cruelly into self-
analysis: turning either to dull indifference,
or unnatural despair. That, in the one tale
fully told, her methods actually led to suicide,
cannot be fairly regarded as the inevitable
result; but something approaching such a
dramatic consequence was happening everywhere.

Miss Dane's power as an artist, however,
does not arise from the logical truth of her
remorseless conclusions; but from the fact that
she has woven a story of vivid interest to every

reader, actually reflecting many most interesting aspects of character, from an educational
tract, where all the persons and events are
centred upon an institution to which men are
forbidden entry, and where life is solely
directed towards the class-rooms, only divided
into successive school terms, and wholly
regulated by the school bell.

But, as we have already suggested, Miss
Dane is not burdened with any concrete message to mankind. We need not seek after
one consistent interpretation for her work.
Her main concern is with the art of creation,
the means for picturing life, the craft of fiction.
" Legend " we recognise as a triumph in
workmanship; but on more ordinary back-
grounds she achieves a similar success. The
supposed " collaborator " intrudes tiresomely
upon a few pages of " First the Blade "; but,
with this trivial exception, we find her tech-
nique everywhere most competent. She repro-
duces, or re-makes, living people of strong
personality; whose humanity is instinctive.
Her output, so far, is varied judiciously: the
sleepy village existence of Justin and Laura:
the stifling atmosphere of Clare's school life:
and the " arty " flavour beloved of Miss Serle.
She is humourous in description, brisk in narrative, dramatic in dialogue.

But, in the end, I am disposed to discover
her chief excellence as an artist, in the triumphant avoiding of over-elaborate analysis,

while achieving real subtlety. Pre-eminently in "Legend," but no less surely in all her work, Miss Dane leans heavily upon the hint. She demands from her readers quick response to a suggestion. She does not provide much movement. Yet she never wearies you, or wastes herself upon that wilderness of the unfinished sentence, that perpetual starting to say something which seems better not spoken, that infinitely protracted questioning of the soul; which is the besetting sin of her contemporaries. Most modern novelists never leave their characters alone for one moment. They are for ever pulling them to pieces, turning them inside out. They scarcely seem certain that anyone—in fiction or in real life —actually exists.

Miss Dane is fortunately content to suffer her people to speak, and act, for themselves. Having brought them to life, she lets them go their own way, so to speak. As a result they fit into the universe. They exist for us: laughing, struggling, or suffering; weak or strong, clever or stupid; even as we are: a gift worthy of gratitude to Man from Art.

THE REGIMENT OF WOMEN 1917
FIRST THE BLADE - - 1918
LEGEND -   -   -   - 1919

MARY FULTON

MARY FULTON

Miss Fulton is primarily a character-analyst, and she indulges, far more than most of her contemporaries, in general reflections on life. In fact, her comments upon the War, and its effects on character, reveal a defined attitude towards the whole question.

Probably, however, the welcome accorded to " Blight " was largely due to its somewhat cynical presentation of pre-war Society: for, though published in 1919, we do not here find any allusion, or even consciousness, of the "state of Europe." It is the story of how many lives may be ruined by those (men or women) who, without being precisely vicious, are "merely irresponsible," and, in consequence, "leave an incalculable *blight*" in their train.

Baird, the male doemon, is a familiar type: " One of those smiling, idle, smart men who are to be found in the capital of every country in Europe, whose amorous foppishness " disturbs many women. He is incurably selfish, immoral, but never indecorous; too lazy and too cold for the dangers of passion, but never hesitating to indulge himself at the expense of others. Only his inbred cynicism and indifference towards serious thought, carry him happily over the surface of life: sparkling and debonair, flattered and idle; ruthless in the pursuit of pleasure. He is, indeed, never coarse; and, often, by reason of his detached mental balance, curiously sympathetic and tactful. For a single interview, a delicate situation, one might almost call him a good friend. He never desires to hurt, and, if convenient, will readily help: being a clever enough fellow, superficially: endowed with a pleasant manner and quick understanding.

The beautiful typist, Grace Manners, is far more complex: though, in another sense, she is absolutely primitive. Possessing, in all its fullness, the allure of sex; she yet ought, as Baird told her, "to have been born a man."

"You're too good to be happy when you're naughty, and too naughty to be happy when you're good. It's all a question of temperament. You've got too much: it forces you into the wrong situations. Most people haven't enough: it keeps them where they are."

A really good woman "knew that Grace was one of those people who pass like a meteor through life, kind, generous, emotional, and volatile, yet leaving behind them a trail of sorrow carelessly inflicted, more agonizing than that caused by the most hardened and wicked of reprobates." She, too, left a *blight*.

Yet one can love this girl, where one feels only contempt for Baird. Because she did care, not for herself alone. However transitory her emotions, her sympathy, or her repentance: they were genuine and sincere. She was thoughtfully loyal to her class, in spite of her own luck. She falls in love, passionately, and with complete abandon. To each man she offers herself, nay, implores him to take her —without reserve. It is always " I adore everything in you. Just let me love you. That's all I want. Always and always."

With Baird, it proved no more than an episode—for both: though he, of course, left her more easily; and the separation was her first tragedy, one of short, intense, bitterness. Sir Peter Wren was quite different. He was no less infatuated; but, from the first, he would give all, care for her with a proud, tender, devotion, make her his queen: whereat she was frankly puzzled. " That he should wish to marry her when she had all but offered herself to him was beyond her reasoning." Yet she loved him, loved still more the beautiful things he could give her, the dainty luxury with which he enveloped her bright youth; only, afterwards, youth called to youth; and in a few weeks of delirium with the boy Masters, she realises what life might have given

her. But it is too late. Now it is she who
draws back: knowing she had not real love.
Without faith in herself or in love, she doesn't
want to be worried with things any longer.

Nevertheless, Grace is not without character. Believing we might all be happy, "if
we were as simple and as fine, as the beasts
in our animal relationships," she does, yet
understand herself.

"Oh, I know I am a fool, but I can't help
it. I can't wait and let things take their
natural course. I can't stand mute, and see
people wanting what I've got to give. Then
I seem to melt. I've no head for the future.
It all goes pot. It's silly; still, Life's silly.
Where does it lead? What's it for?"

At bottom, her impetuous abandon, however
reckless and inconsiderate, has a foundation
of generosity. And though—in this instance,
for example—her husband knew nothing, that
"didn't prevent her from feeling she'd been
a thief." She still loved Sir Peter, in a way,
she had a conscience, she hated cynicism, and
could never become callous.

The young clergyman is not much astray in
his definition of "a bad woman":

"They aren't bad, they're unbalanced. You
can only say a thing is bad which is rotten all
through. Now women aren't like that, even
the worst of them. They're all moments,
ideals, impulses. Uncontrolled is the word.
Evil conquers when our inclinations are

stronger than our reason. Unrestrained inclinations lead us always to misery and disillusion. Reason is the goddess of wisdom
holding in her hand the clear light of foresight
and moderation. Women swayed by inclina-
tion are not bad, but piteous, unfortunate,
degenerate.''

The expression, perhaps is priggish: but I
take it Miss Fulton accepts this philosophy,
which—indeed—she is concerned to illustrate.

Always, it seemed, Grace knew her own
nature: '' She must be loved. Every attribute
of her brain, of her heart and of her senses
craved for the embrace and the desire of a
strong, masterful lover. The deep unswerving
affection which her husband had conceived for
her left her almost unmoved. She yearned
for the caress, the intoxication of Love's
highest manifestation.''

He must be masterful. Of Baird, she had
felt '' so much his slave that if he had whipped
her, she would have fawned upon him ''; and
if Sir Peter '' had discovered, if he had been
suspicious, and had whipped her, she would
have adored him.''

Miss Fulton, we see, attributes similar
feelings to the aristocratic Sally in '' The
Plough ''; who tells her lover:

'' You want all of me, although you want
none of me. I must just be all yours, lying
on your door-mat, to tread on and wipe your
feet on.''

Similar instincts in Grace's mother again produced the opposite result.

"There's only one thing that can make life worth while to a woman, and that's a man, a man and his children. Your father drank, and deceived me right from the first. I always knew, and I always forgave him—I had to— he belonged to me."

The type, or perhaps one should say the individual, is certainly full of interest; and Miss Fulton has been skilful enough to make her really attractive. If she, herself, belongs to all time, only a modern writer could have faced such facts, and analysed her with success.

This does not, moreover, exhaust the interest of "Blight," for contrasted with the evil influences exerted, not quite consciously or deliberately, by Baird and Grace ; we have, on the one hand, Irene Redfern, the good woman of strong character, and on the other her sister, Elsi, a spoilt child of society. Irene is a fine ideal, though very human. Her standards and instincts are all her own, curiously aloof from the atmosphere in which she lives, and yet in tune with the best which others, too, might have drawn from it. She loses everything, and gains all. Because to the courage for sacrifice she unites sympathy and devotion to those weaker than she. There are no heroics in her composition: she does effect reform; but her service is patient, faithful, and enduring, built for the conquest of

her own despair. Elsi is far more ordinary;
though we hope rather exceptional in her
depravity. Never trained by suffering or the
necessity for self-restraint; she becomes
gradually more and more unprincipled: and
by indulging her passions without thought or
feeling, slips into the very abyss of sin that
has no palliation from temptation: wrecking
her own life, her husband's, and her sister's.

"The Plough" follows rather similar lines,
though here almost every detail of the plot is
founded on war conditions; and we meet with
a great deal of what may be called war-philo-
sophy; or politics, national and international.

"I suppose if people did know much about
each other there'd never be any wars," concludes the heroine. England "isn't a country," says her friend, "it's a vast bye-election.
Patriotism is a gilt-edged security for poli-
ticians to trade on, that's all. There's one
thing the Englishman doesn't own, although
he governs half the world, and that's that little
island named England. That's the property
of the central offices, and the central hacks.
The Colonials still believe in it, but that's
about all. . . ."

The Empire is dismissed still more cynical-
ly:

"Just as Kultur sighs to be the ultimate
salvation of a decadent Europe: we say the
savages don't make sufficient use of their
mineral wealth. Then we send out an ex-

pedition, and, after a hopeless but splendid
attempt at resistance by unarmed natives, we
add another few thousand square miles to the
Empire. A few more widows on the Pension
List, a few more fatherless children . . .
the capitalists have yet more markets for them
to monopolise, to the disinterest of the British
working man who has fought and survived for
them.''

Ireland, on the other hand, is ''like the
heart of a child, difficult to enter, but impossible to quit''; and the Irishman can always ''reverence that which he neither com-
prehended nor desired to comprehend, this
unshakeable faith of his in that which the
priest had told him, and which without questioning, or reasoning, he had accepted and
would accept until the grave closed over him.''

Americanism, however, does not improve
the Celt. His charming wife had the '' defects
of her qualities. She could like nothing without wanting to Americanise it. She was
forced, against sentiment, to,—as it were,—
encrust everything she loved with herself, her
money, and through these two mediums, her
country. And the pity was, she was encrust-
ing not only his home, his atmosphere, but
his very personality, with this same meticulous
over-perfected hard perfection.'' '' Americans
were always putting people against them when
they most wanted to make friends.''

Like Miss Richardson, on the other hand,

Miss Fulton dwells on "the secret of the
Germans. Music. No race understands music
in the German sense. It's the key to their
souls. A wonderful, a splendid power of concentration . . . it explained their greatness, their bloody sensuousness, just as the
music of the Russians explained their drunken
savageries, their exotic simplicities."

Finally, the old Victorian, Lady Querin, is
able to pronounce:

"I'd thought of the war as the beginning
of the end, but now it's all over I see it was
merely the end of a great beginning. . . .
You children have been wonderful. Have we
deserved you? . . . But you were born of
us. You made life glorious, but we gave you
life . . . and it has been our rod as well
as our sceptre."

Elder people had seemed "ungrateful and
uncomprehending " because their souls were
helpless; "awkwardly eager to be understanding and understood."

It had been the shibboleth that in social
advancement lay happiness, the determination
that their children should begin where they
had left off. "That was at once the curse
and crown of the Victorians."

Yet Miss Fulton is not merciful to her own
generation:

"These moderns were moral in spite of the
Ten Commandments, and chiefly on eugenic
principles, girls did just what they liked; their

lives were dangerous, often doubtful, but men married them in spite of, or even because of it. . . . . It was the same with material things. Now they were simply ripping, decent, gorgeous, awfully dinky, but not one of these extravagant phrases conveyed anything like the fixed standard of value of the one word *good*."

Of this change, we hear more emphatically, if less decorously, in " Blight ":

" Girls seem to want as much freedom as men nowadays, and they can't be like men really, because once they start acting the giddy goat, they don't know when to leave off: they seem to get a crank in their minds, they can't think of anything else. A man only goes on the loose for fun, or because he's drunk, or just feels like it. But women of to-day, mere girls, most of them, are quite crazy, unless they're strait-laced." We have, indeed, left behind " the generation when people had some semblance of a conscience in their outlook upon life. . . . Nowadays, people had neither hearts, brains, nor souls, but merely gross plebeian appetites. They thought neither of the future, nor of the past. All their energies were centred upon extracting the utmost of pleasure out of the present."

Again, like Miss Macaulay, she has discovered that rich people, most eager for progress, " have done nothing really but talk and talk."

I have dwelt, at length, upon these social and political philosophies because they dissociate Miss Fulton from much of the most characteristic attitude adopted towards Life and fiction by her contemporaries. She offers us conclusions, not reflections, nor observations. She stands outside her characters; which she has definitely created, to illustrate her own, external, experience. They act and speak as we know our friends do act and speak, as we see and meet them—on the surface. She does not attempt to search their souls, to find the ego which words hide. I am not suggesting that this is inferior art; but it is essentially different.

What she attempts, however, Miss Fulton does well : with insight, humour, and dramatic effect.

But, perhaps just because of the mental vigour and alertness, with which she works along her appointed line, the characters are all more or less exponents of her own theories and opinions. They are just not quite themselves.

This is most obvious in the case of Grace Manners, who, clever and shrewd as she was, could never have used the actual language attributed to her. The following utterances, for example, do not become a typist, however familiar with the best people.

" It is a strange thing how people of your class are obsessed with racial forethought, and yet this country of which you're such an integral part, can't even support you. All your youth, and strength, and ideals must go to enrich some foreign land."

" Inwardly, however, I rather terrified him by my disclosures. Insensibly, future possibilities began crowding in upon his brain. He felt apprehensive, while he was pretending to be least affected by what I said." There spoke the schoolmaster or the lecturer : not so much in the thought, but in the word.

Moreover, the philosophy which I have epitomised from these novels, is taken out of the mouths of different characters. Yet it discloses the author.

Miss Fulton, by the way, should remember that the " Serpentine " is *not* in St. James' Park; and should correct this sentence : " Forty is a man's most dangerous age, especially a man like him."

BLIGHT - - 1919
THE PLOUGH - 1919

HOPE MIRRLEES

HOPE MIRRLEES

" Madeleine," " a first novel," by Miss Hope
Mirrlees, belongs to the small group of " historical " novels by women. Women have
seldom taken kindly to this form of fiction,
though there are a few notable exceptions.
And to-day, certainly, they appear less than
ever attracted by the past.

Its position among contemporary novels,
however, is more clearly marked by its author's
assumption, or declaration, that " art and
life are poles apart." The work is based
upon a flat contradition of all realism : yet,
certainly it is not romantic.

" Life," says Miss Mirrlees, " is like a blind
and limitless expanse of sky, for ever dividing
into tiny drops of circumstances that rain down,
thick and fast, on the just and unjust alike.
Art is like the dauntless, plastic force that
builds up stubborn, amorphous substance cell
by cell, into the frail geometry of a shell."

To express the idea more simply, " Life is

the province of free-will, Art the province of fate," which, in practice, means this. You may describe a young girl like *Madeleine*, for example, governed absolutely by certain emotions, influenced exclusively by certain experiences; thereby developing her character along certain lines. At least, for the time being, she is moulded, and—as it were—enveloped, by these thoughts and these circumstances, which combine to build up her character.

Now, in actual life, the stage of growth here presented, might prove to be temporary, no more than an episode. She might, without violence to human nature, have passed through this phase (which is, as it happens, quite immature), and grown up into a, more or less, normal woman, who could find happiness where others enjoyed it. As Miss Mirrlees herself says :—
" In the outer world Madeleine might with time have jettisoned the perilous stuff of youth and have sailed serenely the rough, fresh sea of facts."

But, on the other hand, in the strict logic of ideas, to ensure consistency, to point the moral, to follow up certain revelations of temperament, Madeleine could only complete herself in one place—a lunatic asylum. Destiny, fate, her own nature, and the circumstances forming the plot of this tale, were all leading up, plainly and irresistibly, to that climax. " In the inner world," says Miss Mirrlees, " there was one thing, and one thing only, that could happen to her."

The novelist, you see, conceives of Life as the " outer world," where " there is nothing but the ceaseless, meaningless drip of circumstances "; where, in fact anything may happen : of Art as the " inner world," where " there is a silent, ineluctible march towards a predestined climax "; where, in fact, the " consequences " are inevitable.

And in fiction, which is " the meeting-point of Life and Art," the action must close " completely on the stage of the inner world." That is, the novelist must follow Art—not Life.

It would be impossible, I think, to imagine an ideal for the novel, more fundamentally opposed to the practice and theory of Miss Mirrlees' contemporaries; in whose work we have found a new realism, a final attempt to *identify* Life and Art, to present Reality as it exists within us.

Yet, curiously enough, Madeleine herself is almost a replica of Miss Delafield's " Zella," the young truth-seeker. Both are born *poseurs*, always thrusting themselves into the limelight, seeking to shine by conforming eagerly with the suggestion of the last speaker, perpetually absorbed in the pursuit of a model. Both achieve sincerity by the very passion of imitation. They desire so intensely to be, and to seem, the queen of their chosen circle, that their very acting becomes natural.

In one way, Madeleine is more self-conscious and more analytic; because she is
always attempting to philosophise. She
strives, as Zella did not, to interpret both God
and the world, in the light of her own
emotions.

"In this book, Madeleine sees the trivial,
disorderly, happenings of her life as a
momentous battle waged between a kindly
power who had written on tablets of gold before the world began that she should win her
heart's desire; and a sterner and a mightier
power who had written on tablets of iron that
all her hopes should be frustrated, so that,
finally, naked and bleeding, she might turn to
Him. And having this conception of life, all
her acquaintances become minor *daimones*,
friendly or hostile, according as they seem to
serve one power or the other."

It is true, of course, that fantastic philosophy
was the fashion of her age : but this idea of herself as the peculiar preoccupation of Provid-
ence, offers an admirable excuse for utter
selfishness and scorn of her fellow-creatures :
not inconsistent with adoration of the elect.
Nor does she hesitate to a superstitious observ-
ance of omens, based on chance words and
actions of those whom she despises : "The
spoken word carried for her always a strange
finality." "Talk about *me*," she cries, " or I
shall go mad " : the very epitome of the egoist.

Like Zella, again, Madeleine has charm,

simply because she is so completely a child,
so genuinely—and impulsively—absorbed in
her own one passionate desire—for the friendship and admiration of Mademoiselle de
Scudéry, around which the whole plot revolves. The seventeenth century setting,
moreover, affords Miss Mirrlees abundant
opportunity for the exercise of a fine literary
imagination. She positively revels in the
style of the period; its stilted language, its
fantastic philosophies, its preposterous conventions in narrative, its wild fashions, its
piety, its paganism, its hollow morality : all
essentially artificial.

Madeleine, like all around her, played continually with the idea of God. At one moment,
He seems intent on thwarting her every desire;
at another, specially engaged in arranging the
world for her happiness. Often, a loving
object of adoration, no less seldom a Being to
hate and defy. When all things seem pro-
ceeding as she would have them :—

" The Lord was indeed on her side   .   .   .
in a flash God became at once glorious and
moral—a Being that cares for the work of His
hands, a maker and keeper of inscrutable but
entirely beneficent laws, not merely a daeimon
of superstitious worship."

But stay! Was she accepting His benevo-
lence in a right spirit : " She caught sight of
the crucifix, and she was suddenly filled with
terror. Was this the way to receive the great

kindness of Christ? in having got her the invi-
tation? Really, it was enough to make Him
spoil the whole thing in disgust. She crossed
herself nervously and threw herself on her
knees. At first there welled up from her heart
a voiceless song of praise and love . . .
but this was only for a moment, then her soul
dropped from its height to the following
Litany :—
' Blessed Virgin, Mother of our Lord, make
    me shine on Thursday.
  Guardian Angel that watchest over me,
    make me shine on Thursday.
  Blessed Saint Magdalene, make me shine on
    Thursday.
  Blessed Virgin, Mother of our Lord, give
    me the friendship of Mademoiselle de
    Scudéry.
  Guardian Angel, that watchest over me,
    give me the friendship of Mademoiselle
    de Scudéry.
  Blessed Saint Magdalene, give me the
    friendship of Mademoiselle de Scudéry.'
She gabbled this over about twenty times.
Then she started a wild dance of triumphant
anticipation. It was without a plot, as in the
old days; just a wallowing in an indefinitely
glorious future."
  All her prayers are the same : "Oh!
Blessed Lady, let me cut an exceedingly brave
figure on Thursday. Give me occasions for
airing all the conceits I prepare beforehand.

Make me look furiously beautiful and noble,
let them all think me *dans le dernier galants*,
but mostly *her*.   Give me the friendship of
Mademoiselle de Scudéry."

Her determination to be loved by the popu-
lar, and flattered, authoress of *Le grand Cyrus*,
forms the plot.   Her complete failure in this
enterprise reveals her destiny.   One might
almost say that the whole story leads up to,
and is composed of, her two interviews with
the great lady : when she is prostrated by
nervousness, and makes a sad impression,
whether talking or silent.   Other chapters con-
tain only the girl's exalted hopes and feverish
preparations for the great event.

Miss Mirrlees, indeed, has arranged her
atmosphere with great skill.   The dialogue is
very witty, after the quaint affectations of the
period : the minor characters are drawn with
spirit : many strange customs and ideas are
dramatically described.

Madeleine, for example, is constantly tortured by the provincialisms and bourgeois
manners of her genial father :—

" His habit of expectorating disgusted
her : ' He doesn't even spit high up on the
wall like a grand seignoir,' she would say
peevishly."   Or again :—" Jesus!   His pro-
vinciality!   It was at least ten years since it
had been fashionable to praise a lady's
breasts! "

We have, too, graphic pictures of fine ladies

and gallant courtiers, close imitations of the
De Scudéry, with which Madeleine indulges
her imagination, clever sketches of an infant
prodigy, and shrewd sceptical philosophies
from Jacques, the student, who loves Madeleine, alternately teasing and helping her.

I am disposed to question, however, whether
Madeleine's excessive, and perpetual, self-
analysis, is quite in the period! Its artificial
ideals (composed of false art, sensuous re-
ligiosity and glib psychology), might easily
produce girls like her, and ruin them : but the
constant reasoning about oneself, taking stock
of one's position at every turning, belongs to
our own age. No doubt human nature *was*
like this in the 17th century : but it neither
knew, nor thought, quite so much about itself.

Nevertheless, " Madeleine " is a very striking first novel. As historical fiction it is exceptionally clever: and the theories of Art
and Life, propounded and illustrated by
Miss Mirrlees, have especial interest as a
studied contrast to those inspiring her contemporaries. There is room for both.